CAMBRIDGE
UNIVERSITY PRESS

CAMBRIDGE ENGLISH
Language Assessment
Part of the University of Cambridge

Updated
Second Edition

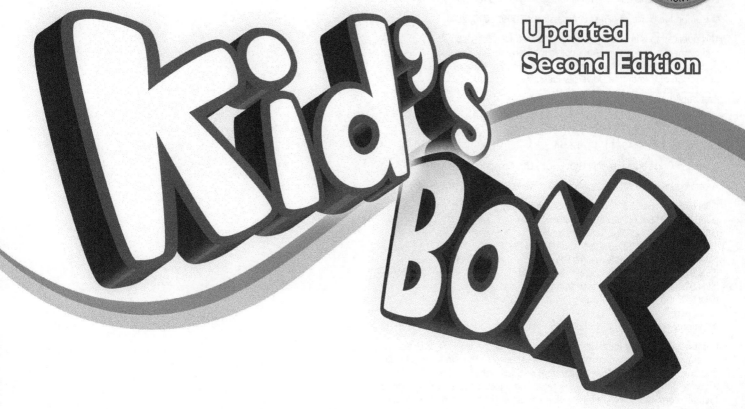

Kid's Box

T0372777

Workbook 5
with Online Resources
American English

Caroline Nixon & Michael Tomlinson

Cambridge University Press & Assessment
www.cambridge.org/elt

Cambridge Assessment English
www.cambridgeenglish.org

Information on this title: www.cambridge.org/9781316627211

© Cambridge University Press & Assessment 2009, 2015, 2017

First published 2009
Second edition 2015
Updated second edition 2017

20 19 18 17 16 15 14 13 12 11

Printed in Great Britain by CPI Group (UK) Ltd, Croydon CR0 4YY

A catalogue record for this publication is available from the British Library

ISBN 978-1-316-62721-1 Workbook with Online Resources 5
ISBN 978-1-316-62755-6 Student's Book 5
ISBN 978-1-316-62704-4 Teacher's Book 5
ISBN 978-1-316-62727-3 Class Audio CDs 5 (3 CDs)
ISBN 978-1-316-62738-9 Teacher's Resource Book with Online Audio 5
ISBN 978-1-316-62791-4 Interactive DVD with Teacher's Booklet 5 (PAL/NTSC)
ISBN 978-1-316-62712-9 Presentation Plus 5
ISBN 978-1-316-63019-8 Posters 5

Additional resources for this publication at www.cambridge.org/elt/kidsboxamericanenglish

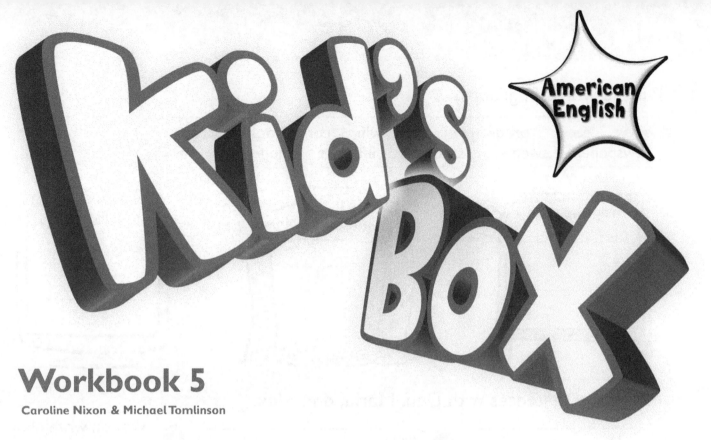

Kid's Box

American English

Workbook 5

Caroline Nixon & Michael Tomlinson

Welcome to our ezine

1 Put the words in groups.

> book   scarf   program   coat   wifi   comic book   screen
> newspaper   sweater   sneakers   Internet   magazine

Things we read
book

Things we wear
scarf

Computer things
program

2 Match the sentences with Dan, Maria, and Alex.

1 I had a nice vacation.   **2** I'd like to write about sports.   **3** We can write about anything in our ezine.

4 I'm new in school.   **5** I live close to Alex.   **6** I didn't know what an ezine was.

 ☐ ☐   1 ☐    ☐ ☐

3 Read and complete.

> ezine   videos   music   store
> ~~magazine~~   Internet   sports   pictures

An ezine is a kind of (1) magazine , but you don't go to the (2) ----------------- to buy it. You can do a search and find it on the (3) ----------------- . You can read about soccer, tennis, and other (4) ----------------- . You can get information about technology and the world around us. You can look at a lot of really interesting (5) ----------------- , listen to all your favorite (6) ----------------- , and watch different kinds of (7) ----------------- . Maria, Dan, and Alex write the new *Kid's Box* (8) ----------------- . They want to win the school ezine competition. There's a great prize!

4 Correct the sentences.

1 An ezine is a kind of book.
No, it isn't. It's a kind of
magazine.

2 You can find an ezine in the store.

----

3 *Kid's Go* is a new ezine.

----

4 The three writers are named Sally, Don, and Alfred.

----

5 There's a prize for the worst ezine.

----

5 Read and order the text.

	ezine for young people. There are
	are Alex, Maria, and
9	Maria likes the natural world and drawing. She
	don't have to go to school.
	things. Alex likes computers and sports, Dan
5	Dan. They all go to the same
	three writers. Their names
1	*Kid's Box* is an exciting new
	school: City School. They all like different
	really loves taking pictures, too. They write
	likes music and clothes, and
	their ezine at the weekend when they

6 Read and complete the questions.

| Where | When | ~~What's~~ |
| Why | How many | What |

1 <u>What's</u> the ezine called?
It's called *Kid's Box*.

2 _____ writers are there?
There are three.

3 _____ 's the ezine about? **It's about the things that they like.**

4 _____ do they write the ezine? **They write it on weekends.**

5 _____ do they write it then? **They write it then because they don't have to go to school.**

6 _____ can you see the ezine? **You can see it on the Internet.**

7 Write the correct sentences.

~~Dan would like~~	oldest of	the country.
Dan	to school	~~music and clothes.~~
Maria walks	are both	Maria.
Alex's the	lives close to	the children.
Alex	~~to write about~~	ten.
Dan and Maria	lives in	every day.

1 <u>Dan would like to write about music and clothes.</u>

2 _____

3 _____

4 _____

5 _____

6 _____

5

8 Choose words from the box to label the pictures.

| geography | language | history | math | dictionary | ~~science~~ | music | exam |

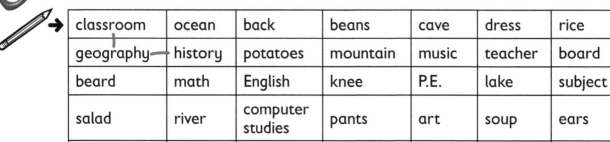

1 **2** **3** **4** **5** **6**

science _____ _____ _____ _____ _____ _____

9 Follow the school words.

classroom	ocean	back	beans	cave	dress	rice
geography	history	potatoes	mountain	music	teacher	board
beard	math	English	knee	P.E.	lake	subject
salad	river	computer studies	pants	art	soup	ears
mustache	pasta	exam	dictionary	science	elbow	field

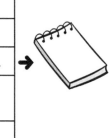

10 Now complete the chart with words from Activity 9.

The body	Food	The natural world
elbow		

Two words don't belong. What are they? _____ _____

Which group are they from? _____

11 Answer the questions.

1 What's your school called? My school is called _____

2 What's your favorite subject? _____

3 What was your first subject yesterday? _____

4 Do you have lunch in school or at home? _____

5 What did you do after lunch yesterday? _____

6 Did you have any homework yesterday? _____

12 Read and complete the school schedule.

- Jim takes these subjects in school: geography, history, music, math, English, P.E., computer studies, art, science.
- English is his last class on Mondays.
- His favorite day is Wednesday. He has P.E. at ten o'clock and music at eleven o'clock. He also has geography in the morning.
- Math is his last class on Tuesdays and Wednesdays.
- On Thursdays his history class finishes at four o'clock, and he has English at eleven o'clock.

- On Mondays he studies a lot. Before lunch he has math after science, and at eleven o'clock he has computer studies. After lunch he first has geography, and then he has history.
- After science on Friday, Jim has these subjects in alphabetical order: history, P.E., computer studies, music, English.
- The first class on Mondays and Fridays is the second class on Tuesdays.
- On Tuesdays the first class is computer studies. Before lunch he has geography, and at two o'clock he has P.E.
- He always has art after lunch, but not on Mondays or Fridays.
- He has music after art on Thursdays.
- He has science four times a week.

	Monday	Tuesday	Wednesday	Thursday	Friday
9:00–10:00				math	science
10:00–11:00					
11:00–12:00					
lunch						
13:00–14:00					
14:00–15:00			English		
15:00–16:00					

13 Now write about Jim's Monday schedule.

On Monday _____

_____

_____

_____

14 Write about the schedule of your favorite school day.

My favorite school day is _____

_____

_____

_____

15 Write the words in the columns.

January ~~children~~ watch village German French bridge dangerous question picture	"ch" (as in **ch**air)	"j" (as in **j**ump)
	children	

16 🔊 11 CD1 Listen, check, and say.

17 Find 17 mistakes in the text.

on mondays i have english, math, and history in the morning. after lunch i only have two classes. they are science and art. art is my favorite subject. on tuesdays i don't have english or math, but i have p.e., which is great. after p.e. i have history and then in the afternoon i have geography and science. i love doing experiments in science.

Punctuation – Capital letters and periods
• Use capital (CAPITAL) letters at the start of sentences and for the names of people (David), the word "I," places (London), days of the week (Monday), and languages (English).
• Use a period (.) at the end of a sentence.

Write it right

18 Now write the text correctly.

On Mondays

19 Write about your dream school schedule.

In my dream school schedule I'd like to have

20 Read and answer.

1 Who's older: Sir Doug or Diggory Bones? <u>Sir Doug is older than Diggory.</u>
2 How long is the model dinosaur? _____
3 What are Diggory's students learning about? _____
4 What did the Rosetta Stone help us do? _____
5 Where was Diggory's computer? _____
6 Who's Emily? _____

21 Read the text. Then look at the code and write the secret message.

Egyptian hieroglyphics were one of the first kinds of writing, but modern people couldn't understand them. Ancient people wrote important things on the Rosetta Stone in three different languages.

In 1822, a very smart man named Jean-François Champollion used two of the languages to understand the third, the Egyptian hieroglyphics. The Rosetta Stone helped us understand the past better.

a	b	c	d	e	f	g	h	i	j	k	l	m

n	o	p	q	r	s	t	u	v	w	x	y	z

<u>V e r y</u> ___ __ __ _____ _____ _____ __ ____ ____

_____. _____ _____ _____ __ _____ _____ _____

____ . ___ _____ __ ____ _____ .

? Do you remember?

1 An internet magazine is called an <u>ezine</u> .
2 We use a _____ to find the meaning of words.
3 _____ is the school subject about different places in the world.
4 In school we learn about plants and the human body in _____ .
5 Two words with a "ch" (as in "<u>ch</u>ildren") are _____ and _____ .
6 At the end of a sentence we use a _____ .

Can do

I can talk about school subjects.
I can ask my friends about their school schedule.
I can use capital letters and periods.

1 Time for TV

What time is it?
It's six o'clock.

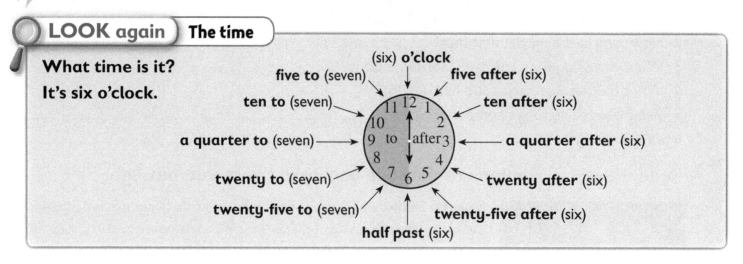

(six) o'clock
five to (seven)   five after (six)
ten to (seven)   ten after (six)
a quarter to (seven) ——→ to | after ←—— a quarter after (six)
twenty to (seven)   twenty after (six)
twenty-five to (seven)   twenty-five after (six)
half past (six)

1 Match the clocks with the pictures.

a ☐   1   2 fun time   3   d ☐

b ☐   4   5 The end   6   e ☐

c ☐   f [1]

2 Write the times.

1 <u>five after</u>
   <u>eleven</u>

2 _____

3 _____

4 _____

5 _____

6 _____

3 Read and draw the times on the clocks.

1 Bill wakes up at 7:10 on Mondays, Wednesdays, and Fridays.
2 Nick leaves home at 8:55 in the morning.
3 Alex sometimes plays soccer at 15:30.
4 Anna always starts her homework at 16:00.
5 Tom watches his favorite show on TV at 18:45 on Tuesdays
   and Thursdays.
6 Sue goes to bed at 21:00 every day.

4 Match the clocks with the sentences for Dan's day yesterday. Put the sentences in order.

a He had lunch at half past twelve. _5_

b Classes started again at a quarter to two. ___

c He caught a bus to school at twenty-five after eight. ___

d School finished at four o'clock. ___

e Dan caught the bus home at ten after four. ___

f Dan got dressed at ten to eight. ___

g He went out to the playground for recess at a quarter to eleven. ___

h Classes began at nine o'clock. ___

5 Find the past of these verbs and write them.

w	a	g	o	t	u	p	u
o	e	y	p	l	k	e	d
k	o	n	u	s	c	j	r
e	i	q	t	o	o	k	a
u	o	p	a	s	y	l	n
p	c	a	u	g	h	t	k
k	b	d	t	i	c	a	f
h	c	a	m	e	h	o	d

go   _went_

come   _____

have   _____

catch   _____

wake up   _____

get up   _____

eat   _____

drink   _____

put   _____

take   _____

6 Answer the questions about yesterday.

1 What time did you get up?
   I got up at _____

2 What time did you go to school?
   _____

3 Where did you have lunch?
   _____

4 What time did you go home?
   _____

5 What did you eat for dinner?
   _____

6 What did you drink in the evening?
   _____

7 Now choose your favorite day of last week and write about what you did.

   _____ _was my favorite day of last week._
   _____
   _____
   _____

8 Choose words from the box to label the pictures.

| series | quiz | cartoon | comedy | ~~weather~~ | sports | news | documentary |

weather _____ _____ _____ _____ _____ _____

9 Write the shows.

1 On this you can see swimming, basketball, tennis, or motorcycle racing. sports _____
2 This show is funny, with funny people. _____
3 We watch this show to see if today is hot or cold. _____
4 This is on every day. It's about important things around the world. _____
5 This show tells us interesting facts about animals, history, and places. _____
6 This show has episodes and can be on TV every day. _____

10 Read and answer the questions.

Channel 1	Channel 2	Channel 3	Channel 4
12:10 *Fun house* (cartoon) 1:00 The news 1:45 The weather 2:15 Chelsea v Milan (soccer) 4:15 *Animals of Africa* (documentary)	11:50 Top songs (music videos) 12:30 *Friendly* (comedy) 2:10 *Count to ten* (quiz) 3:15 Giants v Bouncers (basketball)	12.30 The news 1:05 *Explorers* (documentary) 2:20 *Annie get your gun* (musical comedy movie) 3:45 Cartoon hour	1.15 *Maskman returns* (movie) 2:30 *Our body* (documentary) 3:15 *Answer first* (quiz) 3:55 *Laugh out loud* (comedy)

1 What time is the news on Channel 3? At 12:30. _____
2 What channels are the cartoons on? _____
3 What's on Channel 1 at a quarter to two? _____
4 What are the names of the two quiz shows? _____
5 What are the documentaries about? (1) _____ , (2) _____ , (3) _____
6 What time is the movie on Channel 4? _____

11 Write a TV page with your favorite shows and times.

Channel 1	Channel 2	Channel 3	Channel 4
12:45 Sports today _____	_____ _____	_____ _____	_____ _____

12 **Read and complete the chart.**

Now it's four o'clock. Four friends have a problem because they can't decide which show to watch.

- Sophia's favorite show starts in 20 minutes and is called *Quacky Duck*. She likes cartoons, but doesn't like documentaries or sports shows.
- The other girl, Emma, loves quiz shows.
- *Who wants to be a billionaire?* started at 3:50.

- Frank loves playing sports, and he likes watching it, too. His favorite show starts in 45 minutes.
- The other boy's favorite show is called *World about us*. He's the only child who likes documentaries.
- The documentary starts at ten after four, and the cartoon starts at twenty after four.
- Harry doesn't want to watch *Sunday sports*.
- Finally they all decide to watch Emma's favorite show, but it started ten minutes ago!

Name	Sophia			
Kind of show				
Show name	Quacky Duck			
Show time				

13 **Now answer the questions.**

1 Who doesn't like documentaries? Sophia, Emma, and Frank

2 What's the name of the show they decide to watch? _____

3 When did it start? _____

4 Whose favorite show is it? _____

5 Who doesn't want to watch what's on TV at 4:45? _____

6 When does the cartoon start? _____

14 **Answer the questions.**

1 What's your favorite TV show?
My favorite TV show is _____

2 What kind of show is it?

_____

3 What time is it on?

_____

15 **How many words can you find in "documentaries"?**

star, mice _____

_____

16 Complete the sentences.

| computer | university | ~~review~~ | usually | documentary | beautiful |

1 After you see a movie, you can write a _review_ about it.
2 I _____ wake up at 8:30 in the morning.
3 Let's watch the _____ about monkeys on TV tonight.
4 On Tuesday afternoon the students have _____ studies.
5 My sister is going to _____ next year.
6 Look at Daisy's _____ new jacket!

17 22 CD1 Listen, check, and say.

18 Read the text and answer the questions.

Detective Will Hard is an amazing TV show about a police officer and his adventures. He has to catch dangerous thieves in a big city. He's often in terrible situations. Ben Jones is the actor who plays the police officer. It's on Channel 4 at half past five on Saturday afternoons. I like this show because it's really fast and exciting. There are a lot of action scenes. The show is funny, too. Detective Hard makes a lot of jokes.

Reviews
• A review is about something that you read or saw. You need to describe it and say what you thought about it.

• When you write a review, you need to think about these questions: What? Where? When? Who?

• At the end of the review, you need to think about these questions: Do you like it? Why? / Why not?

Write it right

1 What's the TV show called? _Detective Will Hard._____
2 What's it about? _____
3 Which actor's in it? _____
4 Which channel is it on? _____
5 What time is it on TV? _____
6 Why does he like it? _____

19 Use the questions and answers to write a review of a TV show or movie.

_I'm going to review a_____
_____
_____
_____

20 Read and answer.

1 What's the Baloney Stone? <u>It's a computer program of old languages.</u>

2 Where's the Baloney Stone? _____

3 What time did Emily turn on the TV? _____

4 Which show did Diggory want to watch? _____

5 Who was the cameraman at the college? _____

6 What does Brutus Grabbe want? _____

21 Read the story so far, and then write it in the past.

The story so far ...

Diggory's in a classroom at the college. The reporter and the cameraman arrive. The reporter asks Diggory some questions. Diggory says that he doesn't want the thief to use the Baloney Stone to find treasure. At half past nine Diggory asks Emily to turn on the TV because he wants to watch the news. Brutus Grabbe comes onto the TV screen and laughs. He's the TV cameraman from the college! He wants Diggory's secret password for the computer program.

<u>The story so far ...</u>
<u>Diggory was in a classroom at the</u>
<u>college.</u>
_____
_____
_____
_____
_____
_____
_____
_____
_____

? Do you remember?

1 The time in words is a quarter to eleven. The time in numbers is <u>10:45</u> .

2 The time in numbers is 8:25. The time in words is _____ .

3 A _____ is a TV show that tells us interesting things about our world.

4 Two TV shows that usually make us laugh are _____ and _____ .

5 Two words with a "u" (as in "<u>u</u>sually") are _____ and _____ .

6 At the _____ of the review you write about what you think.

Can do

I can tell the time in English.

I can talk about different kinds of TV shows.

I can write a review of a TV show.

1 Answer the questions.

Cartoon questionnaire

1 What's your favorite comic book? My favorite comic book is _____
2 What's your favorite cartoon movie? _____
3 Do you have any comic books? _____ . What are they called? _____
4 Do you have any cartoon movies? _____ . What are they called? _____
5 Do you like cartoons? _____
6 Can you draw cartoons? _____
7 Do you prefer cartoons or movies with actors? _____
8 Do you think that cartoons and comic books are for grown-ups and children? _____

2 Answer "yes" or "no."

1 The first cartoons were in color. no _____
2 Mickey Mouse was in the first cartoon movie with sound. _____
3 Donald Duck came before Mickey Mouse. _____
4 In the 1970s people used computers to make cartoons. _____
5 The first 3D movie made using computers was *Toy Story*. _____
6 *Shrek* won a prize. _____

3 Plan a report about the history of animation.

Think about the answers to the questions above and about what you learned in the Student's Book.

You need: An introduction   – What you are going to write about
             A middle   – What you learned
             An end   – The most interesting thing you found out

My plan

Introduction	Middle	End
I'm going to write about ...	I learned ...	The most interesting thing I found out is ...

4 Now write your report.

The history of animation
I'm going to write about the history of animation.

5 **Listen and color and write. There is one example.**

2 People at work

People at work

LOOK again   Going to

We use *going to* to talk and write about the future.

Affirmative	Negative (n't = not)	Question
I'm **going to be** a nurse.	He **isn't going to be** a dentist.	**Is** he **going to be** an actor?
She**'s going to visit** me.	We **aren't going to do** it.	**Are** they **going to clean** it?

1 Write the words in the sentences.

| wear | ~~watch~~ | read | play | listen | be |

1 She's going to watch_____ TV after school.
2 He's going to _____ a firefighter when he's older.
3 They aren't going to _____ a comic book.
4 We're going to _____ to pop music.
5 I'm going to _____ my new sneakers.
6 You aren't going to _____ badminton today.

2 Match the questions with the answers.

1	e	2		3		4		5		6		7		8	

1 How are you going to find the street?
2 What time's he going to get up?
3 Where are we going to have lunch?
4 Who are they going to talk to?
5 Which T-shirt are you going to wear?
6 Why's he going to go to the music festival?
7 When's she going to play basketball?
8 What are they going to do after school?

a They're going to talk to their friends.
b I'm going to wear my blue one.
c We're going to have it at home.
d He's going to listen to rock music.
e We're going to look at a map.
f He's going to get up at half past seven.
g They're going to do their homework.
h She's going to play on Saturday.

3 Look at this code. Write the secret message.

	1	2	3	4	5
1	a	b	c	d	e
2	f	g	h	i	j
3	k	l	m	n	o
4	p	q	r	s	t
5	u	v	w	x	y

a = 11, b = 21, c = 31

11-34-51   55-53-15   22-53-42-43-22   54-53   31-53-33-51
A r e   _ _ _   _ _ _ _ _ _   _ _   _ _ _ _

54-53   33-55   14-11-34-54-55?
_ _   _ _ _   _ _ _ _ _?

4 Now write another message for your friend in your notebook.

5 Look at the pictures and answer the questions.

1 What are they going to do? _They're going to wash their clothes._
2 What is she going to do? _____
3 What is he going to do? _____
4 What are they going to do? _____
5 What is he going to do? _____
6 What is she going to do? _____

6 Make negative sentences.

1 _He isn't going to catch the bus._
2 _____
3 _____
4 _____
5 _____
6 _____

7 Look at Sam's calendar for the weekend. Ask and answer the questions.

Friday	morning	School
	afternoon	4 p.m. Play soccer
Saturday	morning	10:45 Visit Grandma
	afternoon	2 p.m. Shopping for pajamas
Sunday	morning	Walk in hills
	afternoon	4 p.m. Movie theater

1 a) Where / Sam / go / Friday morning
   Where's Sam going to go on Friday morning?
b) _He's going to go to school._
2 a) What / Sam / do / Friday afternoon
   _____
b) _____

3 a) What time / Sam / visit his grandma
   _____
b) _____
4 a) What / Sam / buy / Saturday afternoon
   _____
b) _____
5 a) Where / Sam / walk / Sunday morning
   _____
b) _____
6 a) What / Sam / do / Sunday afternoon
   _____
b) _____

8 Choose words from the box to label the pictures.

mechanic	reporter	actor	~~pilot~~
soccer player	dancer	cook	manager

1 pilot

2 _____

3 _____

4 _____

5 _____

6 _____

9 Complete the chart.

person	verb
teacher	teach
	drive
dancer	
	skate
	design
	sing
	paint
	photograph
manager	
tennis player	
runner	
	swim

10 Read and write the words in the puzzle.

1 Someone who drives buses.
  A bus driver_____ .
2 Someone who works with food.
  A _____ .
3 Someone who stops fires.
  A _____ .
4 Someone who takes care of our teeth.
  A _____ .
5 Someone who works in a hospital.
  A _____ .
6 Someone who flies planes.
  A _____ .
7 Someone who repairs cars.
  A _____ .
8 Someone who paints pictures.
  An _____ .
9 Someone who acts in movies.
  An _____ .

1 | b | u | s | d | r | i | v | e | r |
2
3
4
5
6
7
8
9

What's the mystery job? _____

11 Now write a definition for this job.

_____
_____
_____

20

12 These four children are going to have different jobs. Write the numbers.

a ☐ ☐ ☐   b ☐ ☐ ☐   c 1 ☐ ☐   d ☐ ☐ ☐

1 He's going to fly planes.
2 He's going to travel a lot.
3 He's going to repair cars.
4 She's going to use eggs.
5 He's going to get dirty.
6 She's going to wear a white hat.

7 He's going to visit a lot of airports.
8 She's going to work in a kitchen.
9 She's going to take care of people's teeth.
10 He's going to work with machines.
11 She's going to tell children not to eat candy.
12 She's going to wear gloves and a mask.

13 Slim Jim's a famous singer. Read and complete his calendar.

1 He's going to meet his manager after lunch on Friday.
2 The same day that he sings, he's going to open a new school in the morning.
3 He's going to go to the movie theater next Thursday afternoon.
4 After lunch on the day he arrives in London, he's going to talk to some children who are in the hospital.
5 He's going to have a TV interview before lunch on the day he goes to the movie theater.

6 He arrives at London airport next Monday morning.
7 On the same day that he's having dinner with some actors, he's going to visit a music store in the morning.
8 He's going to sing in a big soccer stadium.
9 He's flying to Spain in the morning of the same day that he's going to meet his manager.
10 He's going to have dinner with some actors next Tuesday evening.

	Monday	Tuesday	Wednesday	Thursday	Friday
a.m.	_____	_____	_____	_____	_____
	lunch	lunch	lunch	lunch	lunch
p.m.	_____	_____	_____	_____	meet manager

14 Answer the questions.

1 Where are you going to go after school this afternoon? _I'm going to go_____
2 Who are you going to see this evening? _____
3 When are you going to do your homework? _____
4 What time are you going to go to bed tonight? _____

15 Can you remember? Complete the sentences.

doctor	~~older~~	answer
picture	stronger	treasure

1 The manager is <u>older</u> than the actor.
2 The swimmer is _____ than the writer.
3 The farmer found some _____ .
4 The teacher showed her students a _____ .
5 The _____ is writing on some paper.
6 The dancer knows the _____ .

16 🎵 **36 CD1** Listen, check, and say.

17 Find 13 mistakes in the text.

My dad's job
My dads a cook in a restaurant. Its called Petes Diner. The restaurants big. It has more than 20 tables and five cooks. Dad likes his job, but he doesnt get many vacations. He isnt working today, but hes cooking dinner for me and my sister. He doesnt always cook at home because hes often tired when he finishes work. Moms a great cook, too, but she doesnt get any money for cooking. Shes a history teacher.

Punctuation – The apostrophe
We use an apostrophe:
• to show a letter or letters are missing when we connect two words (*do not* = *don't*, *I have* = *I've*).

• to show possession (*John's book*).

Write it right

19 Write about a job someone in your family does.

My _____ 's a _____
_____
_____
_____
_____
_____
_____
_____
_____
_____
_____
_____

18 Now write the text correctly.

My dad's job
_____
_____
_____
_____

20 Read and answer.

1 What's Diggory's job? <u>He's an archeologist.</u> ....
2 Where does Brutus want Diggory to meet him? ....
....
3 Why did Diggory call him "a pirate"? ....
4 What time are Diggory and Emily going to meet Brutus? ....
5 Is Brutus at the library? ....
6 Who has a letter for Diggory? ....

21 Read and order the text.

has the program, but he wants Diggory's ☐

ancient languages. Brutus Grabbe took it from ☐

The Baloney Stone is a very important computer [1]

secret password. Brutus went on the evening news ☐

at the Old City Library at 10:45, but Brutus wasn't there. ☐

on TV to speak to Diggory. He told him to meet him ☐

program that can help us understand ☐

Diggory's classroom at the college. Now Brutus ☐

? Do you remember?

1 A <u>pilot</u>............ flies planes.
2 A mechanic .... cars.
3 When people have problems with their teeth, they see a ....
4 We use "................ ...." to talk and write about the future.
5 Two words with a short "er" (as in "doct<u>or</u>") are ....
and ....
6 We use an apostrophe to show a .... is missing when we join two words.

Can do   I can use *going to* to talk about the future.
I can talk about people at work.
I can use apostrophes.

23

1 Teeth quiz. Read and choose the right words.

1 The teeth we have when we are young are called
   a) juice teeth.   b) baby teeth.   c) wisdom teeth.
2 How many different types of teeth do we have?
   a) three   b) four   c) five
3 The hard part on the outside of our teeth is called
   a) crown.   b) root.   c) enamel.
4 We use our incisors to
   a) cut our food.   b) chew our food.   c) drink.
5 Molars are at the
   a) side of our mouth.   b) front of our mouth. c) back of our mouth.
6 The part of the teeth in our gums is called
   a) the enamel.   b) the crown.   c) the root.

2 Complete the teeth mind map.

brush for two minutes   baby teeth   drink milk   go twice every year
eat carrots and apples   brush twice a day   permanent teeth   listen
don't drink sugary drinks   rinse with water

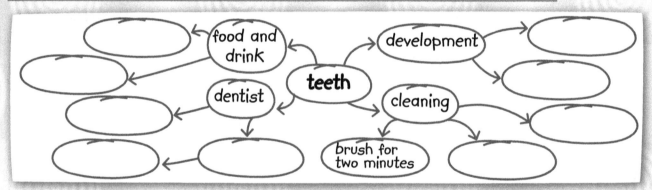

3 Answer the questions.

1 How many teeth do you have? I have _____
2 Do you have any baby teeth? _____
3 How old were you when you got your first permanent tooth? _____
4 Do you like going to the dentist? _____
5 What does the dentist say to you? _____
6 What do you do to take care of your teeth? _____

4 Use the answers to write about your teeth.

My teeth
I have _____ teeth.

5 **Read the letter and write the missing words. Write one word on each line.**

Dear KBTV,

Last Saturday I saw something on your channel
about a new quiz show for young people. It's

Example _called_ .... *Boxing Smart!*
I wrote to you last year about a different
show, but you needed people who were older

1 .... me. I think this new quiz
show is for children of my age, and we have to

2 .... questions about different

3 school subjects. I'm very .... at
geography and history, but science is my best
subject.

4 I would like .... go on the quiz
show. Please can you send me

5 .... more information so that I
can show my parents?

From
Robert Brown

Review Units 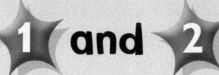 and

1 Read the story. Choose words from the box to complete the sentences.

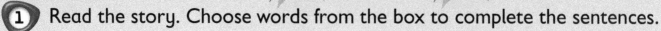

> channel   painted   history   quiz   firefighter   time   going   documentary
> jobs   ~~show~~

Friendly

Friendly is a really funny comedy (1) show_____ . It's on TV at twenty to five every day. In this show there are five friends who all go to the same school in a big city. They live and study at the school, but they aren't all in the same class.

They're all going to have different (2) _____ when they grow up. Peter wants to be a cook, Jenny wants to be an actor, Sally wants to be a taxi driver, Jim wants to be a (3) _____ , and Sue wants to be an artist.

In the story last week, Sue (4) _____ a picture for an art competition, and Jenny sat as a model for her. In the picture that Sue painted, Jenny had one square eye, which was red, and a carrot for a nose. One of her legs was a cell phone and the other was a banana. Sue's friends don't think she's (5) _____ to win the competition, but Sue's happy. She knows she isn't going to be a famous artist!

2 Choose a title for this episode of *Friendly*.

a) Modern art
b) Fun and games
c) Beautiful people

3 Draw and color Sue's painting.

4 Match the questions with the answers.

1	Why do zebras like old movies?			An eggzam!
2	What goes up slowly and comes down quickly?			When there are two of them!
3	What's a chicken's most important test in school?			B.
4	What do you call bears with no ears?		1	Because they're in black and white.
5	What's always slow to come, but never arrives?			An elephant in an elevator!
6	When do elephants have eight feet?			Tomorrow.

5 Complete the sentences. Count and write the letters.

1 An Internet magazine is called an _ezine_____ .

2 The study of the past is called _____ .

3 Eight fifteen is _____ after eight.

4 The class when we draw and paint is _____ .

5 Good, better, _____ .

6 The study of different countries is called _____ .

7 A competition with questions is a _____ .

8 Somebody who repairs cars is a _____ .

9 Something we study in school is called a _____ .

10 A manager works on this in an office. A _____ .

11 Eleven thirty is _____ past eleven.

12 The study of numbers is called _____ .

13 Somebody who paints pictures is an _____ .

14 The opposite of work is _____ .

5

6 Now complete the crossword puzzle. Write the message.

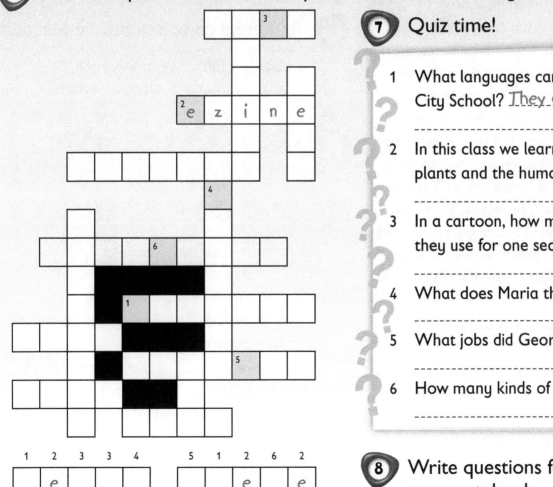

7 Quiz time!

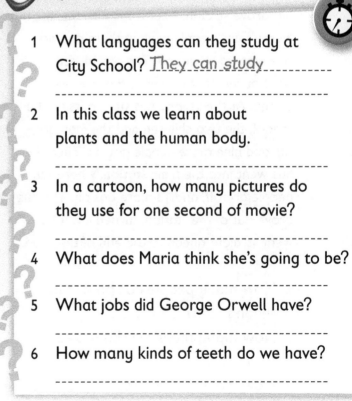

1 What languages can they study at City School? _They can study_____

_____

2 In this class we learn about plants and the human body.

_____

3 In a cartoon, how many pictures do they use for one second of movie?

_____

4 What does Maria think she's going to be?

_____

5 What jobs did George Orwell have?

_____

6 How many kinds of teeth do we have?

_____

8 Write questions for your quiz in your notebook.

3 City life

right ➡ left ⬅ straight ahead ⬆ corner ↰

past ⬆ across ⬆ down ⬅

1 Read and answer the questions.

Yesterday afternoon five people got on a bus at the bus station: one man, two women, and two children. The bus left the station at nine o'clock. It had to stop at the corner because the traffic lights were red. The bus turned left after the traffic lights.

The bus didn't stop at the first bus stop, but drove straight ahead because there weren't any people waiting there and no one wanted to get off. The bus turned right at the next corner and drove over the bridge. At the second bus stop, outside the school, the two children and the man got off, and nine more people got on. Then the bus went into the train station, where ten people got off, and 12 more got on. The bus drove out of the station, turned left, and went straight ahead to the end of the road.

1 How many people got off at the second stop? _____
2 How many times did the bus turn left? _____
3 How many people were on the bus when it drove out of the train station? _____

2 Check (✓) or cross (✗) the sentences.

1 Yesterday morning six people got on at the bus station: two men, one woman, and three children. _____
2 The bus had to stop at the corner because the traffic lights were red. _____
3 After the first bus stop, it turned left at the next corner. _____
4 At the second bus stop, outside the hospital, the two children and the man got off. _____

3 Read and complete the sentences.

down	left	on the corner
straight ahead	right	~~across~~

1 She ran across____ the park.
2 She turned _____ at the corner of Queen Street.
3 He went _____ at the traffic lights.
4 He waited for his friend _____ outside the school.
5 He turned _____ into King Street.
6 He walked _____ Prince Street.

4 Follow the directions and write the message.

London	to	29	places	million	is
of	see	the	interesting	in	and
a lot	are	year	visit	people	every
biggest	There	U.K.	it.	city	the

r = right   l = left   u = up   d = down

London – 5r – 3d – 5l – 4r – 2u – 2l – 2d –1l – 1u – 1l – 1u – 3r – 1u – 2l – 1d – 4r – 1d – 3l – 2u – 2r – 2d – 1l – 1d

London _____ _____ _____ _____ _____ _____

_____ _____ _____ _____ _____ _____

_____ _____ _____ _____ _____ _____

_____ _____ _____ _____ _____ _____

5 Put these buildings on the map.

1 The gym's to the right of the supermarket.
2 The movie theater's across from the bus station.
3 The castle's across from the parking lot.
4 The library's between the café and the toy store.
5 The school's on the other side of the road from the bookstore and across from the hospital.
6 The bookstore's behind the fire station.
7 The stadium's on the other side of the road from the bookstore, on the corner.

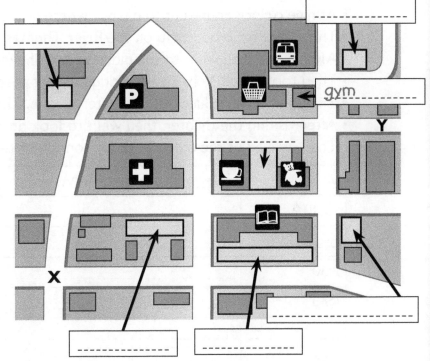

6 Find these buildings in Activity 5.

1 Start at the X. Go straight ahead and take the first road on the right. Go past the hospital and the café. It's the building on the left before the toy store. What is it? _____

2 Start at the X. Turn right and walk to the fire station. Go past the fire station and walk to the next corner. Turn left. It's on the corner on the right. What is it? _____

7 Now write two sets of directions for a friend to follow.

1 Start at the X. Go ...

8 Choose words from the box to label the pictures.

| museum | post office | ~~hotel~~ | airport | restaurant | castle | theater | police station |

1. hotel
2. _____
3. _____
4. _____
5. _____
6. _____

9 Unscramble and write the words.

1 prrtaio   airport
2 eatther   _____
3 letsac   _____
4 aeiiolonpsttc   _____
5 sumemu   _____
6 ethol   _____

10 Complete the chart. Look in the Student's Book to find the names of the places.

Yesterday Paul visited London with his family. They went to seven different places.

• At nine o'clock Paul went to a place where you can see exciting things from all over the world.
• They went for a boat trip on the River Thames at half past ten.
• After lunch they went to the place where Shakespeare and his actors showed their plays.
• They took a cab from Tower Bridge at half past five and went back to their hotel.
• They had a picnic lunch at a quarter to one. They ate some sandwiches in Hyde Park.
• After visiting the theater, they went to look at an old building next to Tower Bridge.
• They arrived at the oldest hotel in London at ten to six. They had dinner and went to bed.

9:00	Went to the British Museum.
10:30	
2:30	
4:30	
5:50	

11 Look at the letters on the clock and write the words.

1 It's five to one.   straight
2 It's eight o'clock.   _____
3 It's ten to six.   _____
4 It's ten after nine.   _____
5 It's twenty-five after four.   _____
6 It's twenty-five to three.   _____

Clock letters: sch, stra, ight, st, p, ark, oad, ool, ore, r, sh, adium

12 Write "who," "that," or "where."

1 A place _where_ you can buy stamps.

2 Someone _____ flies planes.

3 Something _____ you have to buy when you go by bus or train.

4 A place _____ we go to see a play.

5 Someone _____ cooks food in a restaurant.

6 A place _____ you can see old paintings and books.

7 A place _____ you can catch a plane.

8 A place _____ you can get money.

9 Someone _____ repairs cars.

10 A place _____ you go to cross a river.

13 Now find the words from Activity 12.

a	c	e	t	u	r	e	d	p	m
i	q	p	i	l	o	t	b	m	u
r	c	y	c	s	z	a	r	e	s
p	o	s	t	o	f	f	i	c	e
o	b	p	h	d	o	v	d	h	u
r	o	a	e	u	l	k	g	a	m
t	m	k	n	o	a	n	e	n	y
c	a	w	t	k	r	o	t	i	p
f	t	b	r	t	p	i	e	c	o
s	u	c	e	t	i	c	k	e	t

14 Write a definition of these words.

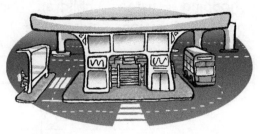

1 A place _____ .

2 Someone _____ .

15 Put these places on your map.

castle   bank   hotel   airport
restaurant   museum   theater

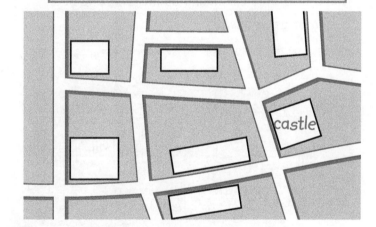

castle

16 Now write directions from the castle to three places on the map.

| 1 | Start at the castle. Go ... |

17 Ask your friend to follow your directions.

31

18 Write the words in the columns.

shopping   listen   children   information   stop   castle   watched   machine
place   question   adventure   directions

"s" (as in **s**un)	"sh" (as in **sh**e)	"ch" (as in **ch**icken)
listen		

19 **10 CD2** Listen, check, and say.

20 Find 14 spelling mistakes in the text.

In this picture we can see a lot of children playeing.
Three boyes are siting on the ground and plying
with their toyes. They have some toy trucks and
a buss. They're close to two ladys who are sitinng
on chairs. These ladys are the boiys' moms. Some
older children are flyng their kites. One boye's kite
is in a tree. He's climmbing up the tree, and he's
trieing to get it down.

Spelling

Nouns	Plurals	Verbs	
toy	toys	enjoy	enjoys
day	days	play	plays
balcony	balconies	cry	cries
shelf	shelves	study	studies
leaf	leaves	watch	watches
box	boxes	drive	driving
		stop	stopping
		run	running
		swim	swimming
		climb	climbing

Write it right

22 Describe your school playground.

On our school playground we can see

21 Now write the text correctly.

In this picture we can see a lot of
children playing.

23 Read and answer.

1 Why was it the wrong library? _Because it was the wrong city._
2 Which city does Brutus mean? _____
3 What are they going to do now? _____
4 What is outside Alexandria? _____
5 What's on the walls of the cave? _____
6 Who's the taxi driver? _____

24 Who said it? Read and match.

1    **2**    **3**    **4**

a I think he means the city of Alexandria in Egypt. `1`

b Brutus can use the Baloney Stone to understand the writing! ☐

c What are we going to do now? ☐

d … can open the door to mountains of secret treasure! ☐

e Now let's get a cab and find a hotel. ☐

f Yes, son. ☐

? Do you remember?

1 An actor sometimes works in a _theater_____ .
2 You can stay in a _____ when you go on vacation.
3 Be careful when you walk _____the road. Look out for cars!
4 The opposite of "turn right" is "turn _____."
5 Two words with a "sh" (as in "she") are _____ and _____ .
6 One leaf, two _____ .

Can do   I can talk about places around town.
I can give and understand directions.
I can spell plural nouns.

Geography Cities

1 City quiz. Read and choose the right words.

1 The capital city of the U.S.A. is   a) New York.   b) Los Angeles.   c) Washington, D.C.
2 Paris is the capital city of   a) Japan.   b) Australia.   c) France.
3 The only city in two continents is   a) Istanbul.   b) Moscow.   c) Cairo.
4 In 1900 the biggest city in the world was   a) Rome.   b) New York.   c) London.
5 The first cities in the world were in
   a) the Amazon Valley.   b) the Indus Valley.   c) the Thames Valley.
6 People started living in cities
   a) to buy and sell food.   b) to catch the bus.   c) because they didn't like farming.

2 Read this report about Stratford-upon-Avon.

Stratford-upon-Avon is a town close to Birmingham in England. About 25,000 people live here. The city is more than 800 years old. It's famous because William Shakespeare was born here. He wrote a lot of plays, including *Romeo and Juliet* and *Macbeth*. You can still see his plays today in the Royal Shakespeare Theater.

There are a lot of other interesting places to go. Children can go to the museum, the library, the sports center, the movie theater, and the park. The town also has a bus and train station. I like Stratford-upon-Avon because the river is beautiful. The only thing I don't like is that it takes a long time to travel to the beach.

3 Complete the Stratford-upon-Avon mind map.

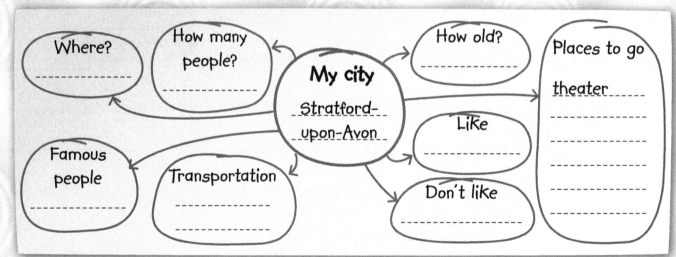

4 Now draw a mind map about your town or city.

5 Use the information from Activity 4 to write your report.

My city

Listen and write. There is one example.

6

George's vacation to London

	Transportation:	by .....train................
1	Hotel name:	The ....
2	Where the hotel is:	next to the British ....
3	Hotel phone number:	....
4	Where George visited:	The .... Theater
5	Time of the play:	Sunday at ....

4 Disaster!

We use the *past progressive* to describe what was happening in the past.

Affirmative	Negative (n't = not)	Question
I **was listening** to music.	You **weren't playing** tennis.	**Was** she **reading**?
They **were walking** to school.	He **wasn't running** in the park.	**Were** they **sailing**?

1 Match the pictures with the text.

Emma's talking to her teacher. She's saying why she was late for school.

☐ Then I saw the bus. It was coming down the street, so I started to run.

☐ The books were on the road in the water when the bus ran over them.

☐ I didn't have a coat or an umbrella, so I decided to get the bus.

☐ Now I can't find my homework. It must be on the road. Sorry! And I'm sorry I'm late!

[1] I had a disaster this morning. I was walking to school when it started to rain.

☐ When I was running for the bus, I dropped my school bag and my books fell out onto the road.

2 Write the verbs in the chart. Look at the spelling.

~~move~~   cut   stop   live   enjoy   wake up
shout   lose   cook   swim   carry   get

tak~~e~~ing (e + -ing)	sail**ing** (+ -ing)	run**ning** (x2 + -ing)
moving		

3 Read and choose the right words.

1 They were sailing across the lake (when) / **because** it started to rain.
2 He was **climb / climbing** in the mountains when it started to snow.
3 My dad was taking a shower when the phone **ring / rang**.
4 The boy **was / were** flying his kite when he hurt his elbow.
5 They were losing **if / when** he scored the goal.

4 Write questions and answers about Paul's day.

1 <u>What was Paul doing at twenty after three?</u>   <u>He was catching the bus.</u>

2 ------------------------------------   ------------------------------------

3 ------------------------------------   ------------------------------------

4 ------------------------------------   ------------------------------------

5 ------------------------------------   ------------------------------------

6 ------------------------------------   ------------------------------------

5 Read and complete the chart.

Last week somebody broke a chair in the classroom during playtime. The children don't want to tell the teacher who broke the chair, so the teacher is trying to find out.

David was wearing a red sweater and a long scarf. Betty was wearing a short skirt and green shoes. Katy was wearing jeans and a T-shirt. William was wearing gray pants and a blue shirt.

One girl was jumping around the classroom. One of the boys was playing soccer outside. One girl was reading a book on the playground. David was talking to his friends on the playground. The child who broke the chair wasn't wearing green shoes or gray pants.

Name	David			
Clothes				
Where?				
What doing?				

Who broke the chair? ------------------------ .

6 Choose dates from the box to label the pictures.

August 26, 1883   ~~November 1, 1755~~   May 6, 1937   April 14, 1912
December 28, 1908   October 10, 1780

November 1, _____ _____ _____ _____ _____
1755 _____ _____ _____ _____ _____

7 Read and write the dates.

1 The day before the twenty-fifth.
The twenty-fourth. _____
2 The day after the twenty-first.
_____
3 The day after the twenty-fourth.
_____
4 This day is three days after the twenty-sixth.
_____
5 This is the day after the twenty-third.
_____
6 This day is three days before the thirtieth.
_____

8 Complete the sentences.

1 The first month is January .
2 The third month is _____ .
3 The fifth month is _____ .
4 The seventh month is
_____ .
5 The eleventh month is
_____ .
6 The twelfth month is _____ .

9 Unscramble and write the months. Put them in order.

~~gjaaum~~   frbryeua   charm   lipar
yam   juen   uyjl   atuugs   restebpem
boorcte   mnborvee   redbeemc

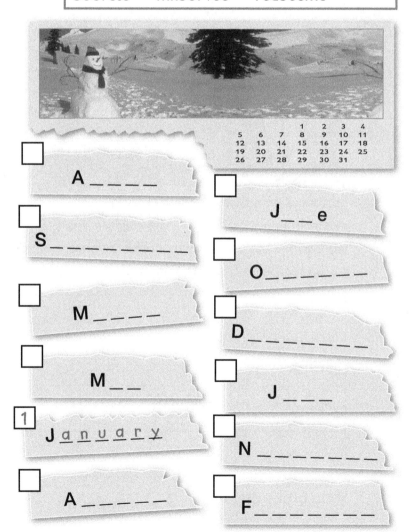

	1	2	3	4
5	6	7	8	9	10	11
12	13	14	15	16	17	18
19	20	21	22	23	24	25
26	27	28	29	30	31

☐ A _ _ _ _

☐ J _ _ e

☐ S _ _ _ _ _ _ _

☐ O _ _ _ _ _ _

☐ M _ _ _ _

☐ D _ _ _ _ _ _ _

☐ M _ _

☐ J _ _ _

1 J a n u a r y

☐ N _ _ _ _ _ _ _

☐ A _ _ _ _ _

☐ F _ _ _ _ _ _ _

10 Answer the questions.

1 What date was it yesterday? It was _____

2 What date is it going to be next Saturday? _____

3 When's your birthday? _____

4 When's your friend's birthday? _____

5 When's your teacher's birthday? _____

6 On what date does school finish this semester? _____

11 Match the words with the pictures.

1 storm   **2** tsunami   **3** ice   **4** hurricane

5 volcano   **6** fog   **7** fire   **8** lightning

12 Now match the words and pictures with the definitions.

a Heavy rain and strong winds. [1]

b Very cold water that is solid, not liquid.

c A mountain with a big hole at the top through which liquid rock and hot gas can come out.

d Electricity in the air that passes from one cloud to another or to the ground.

e Burning material and gases that can burn other things.

f A cloud that is close to the ground or the ocean.

g An enormous and fast wave.

h This is the worst kind of storm, with very strong winds and heavy rain.

13 Keep a weather diary.

Date		sun	wind	cloud	storm	rain	snow	fog
Monday	_____							

14 Write the words in the columns.

| story | ~~storm~~ | disaster | terrible | stopped | wanted | decided | dangerous |

❶ ●	❷ ●●	❸ ●●●	❹ ●●●●
storm			

15 🔊 22 CD2 Listen, check, and say.

16 Find the 22 simple past and past progressive verbs and 4 sequencing words in this story.

My favorite movie of the year (was) *Detective Will Hard 2*. This is what (happened) in the most exciting scene of the movie.

The thieves (were running) after Detective Hard. He (had) to jump off a really high building to escape. (Then) he jumped onto a truck, which was full of black plastic bags, but the bad guys got onto a motorcycle and started to follow him. The motorcycle was much faster, so it wasn't long before it was next to the truck on the road. One of the thieves was trying to climb up the side of the truck when Hard jumped off it and onto the back of the motorcycle. The driver and Hard were fighting as they went over a bridge. Then Hard pushed the driver off the motorcycle into the river. After that he quickly stopped the motorcycle before it hit a bus. Next he called another police officer on his cell and pulled the thief out of the river. He said, "Water you doing here?" Everybody laughed.

Write it right

Reviews
- When we write a story, we think about what happened, where and when it happened, and who was there. For this we use verbs in the simple past.
- Then we describe what was happening at the same time. This makes the story more interesting. For this we use verbs in the past progressive.
- We use connecting words like *and*, *but*, and *because*. We also use sequencing words like *then*, *next*, and *after that*.

17 Answer the questions.

1 What was the movie called? _Detective Will Hard 2_
2 Where was Detective Hard at the beginning of the scene? _____
3 What was happening as they went over the bridge? _____
4 Who fell in the river? _____
5 What happened at the end of the scene? _____
_____

18 Write about a scene from your favorite movie.

My favorite movie is called ...

19 Read and answer.

1 What does "Canis Major" mean? <u>It means "the big dog."</u>
2 What's the brightest star called? _____
3 What was the date in the story? _____
4 When did Diggory remember the disaster? _____
5 What destroyed ancient Alexandria? _____
6 What came after the volcanic eruption? _____

20 Complete the sentences from the story. Match them with the pictures.

light	~~date~~	dangerous
hot	storm	secret

1 What's the <u>date</u> today, Emily?
2 Night's falling, and a _____'s coming.
3 Is it too _____ for you, Bones?
4 Today, it's going to show us the "'opening" of the _____ cave!
5 It's really _____ down here.
6 Run to the _____ , Emily!

? **Do you remember?**

1 It's very difficult to see when the weather is <u>foggy</u> .
2 We sometimes see _____ in the sky when there's a storm.
3 Today's date in numbers is _____ .
4 Tomorrow's date in words is _____ .
5 Two words that have stress on the first syllable are _____ and _____ .
6 We use connecting words like _____ and _____ when we tell stories.

Can do
I can talk about the weather and disasters.
I can talk about things that were happening in the past.
I can tell a story.

1 Disasters quiz. Read and choose the right words.

1 Natural disasters happen because of
a) people.   b) land moving.
c) natural forces.

2 Earthquakes and tsunamis happen close to
a) plate boundaries.   b) rock.
c) crust.

3 Earthquakes happen when plates move
a) slowly.   b) all day.   c) suddenly.

4 The Richter scale is used to measure
a) hurricanes.   b) earthquakes.
c) tsunamis.

5 A tsunami is a lot of enormous
a) fish.   b) earthquakes.   c) waves.

6 Most tsunamis occur in the
a) Atlantic Ocean.
b) Pacific Ocean.   c) Indian Ocean.

2 Choose words from the box to complete the text.

boat	earthquake	underwater	Ocean	dangerous
hours	~~Japanese~~	hundred	rock	minutes

The word "tsunami" comes from the (1) Japanese word meaning "harbor wave." A tsunami happens when a lot of water is moved under the ocean by an (2) _____ , volcano, or other disaster. Most tsunamis are because of (3) _____ earthquakes, but not all earthquakes cause tsunamis – an earthquake has to be over 6.75 to cause a tsunami. Nine out of ten tsunamis happen in the Pacific (4) _____ . A tsunami can travel at seven (5) _____ kilometers an hour. When a tsunami hits land, it can be very (6) _____ .

3 Find out about a volcano, tsunami, or earthquake. Make notes about it.

	What?
	Where?
	Facts:
	Disaster:

4 Now use the information to write your report.

My report

Emma's talking to her friend David about what he did last night.
What does David say to Emma?

Read the conversation and choose the best answer.
Write a letter (A–E) for each answer.

There is one example.

Example

 Emma: Did you watch TV last night?

 David: D..

Questions

1 **Emma:** What did you watch?

   David: ....

2 **Emma:** What was it about?

   David: ....

3 **Emma:** Really? Was there anything on earthquakes?

   David: ....

4 **Emma:** What time did it finish?

   David: ....

A Yes, there was. It was really amazing.

B I watched a documentary.

C It wasn't late. It finished at 7 o'clock.

D Yes, I did. **(Example)**

E It was all about natural disasters.

43

Review Units  and

1 Read the story. Choose words from the box to complete the sentences.

left	~~March~~	straight	walking	restaurant	quarter	wasn't	corner
theater	were	right					

Friendly

Last Saturday, (1) _March_ 30, was Jim's birthday. He decided to go to the city center with Peter to have lunch in an expensive (2) _____ and to go to the theater to see a movie. They went to the station at a (3) _____ after nine on Saturday morning and caught the train from platform 1. They didn't know the city very well, and they didn't have a map, so they decided to explore. When they were walking down a long road, they turned (4) _____ , not right, and got lost. When they were trying to find the right street, they saw hotels, post offices, gyms, and museums, but no restaurants. At ten after two, they found a small café. They were really hungry, so they stopped there and had a burger and fries for lunch. When they got to the movie theater, they found it (5) _____ showing the action movie they wanted to see – it was showing a cartoon about funny animals for very young children.

They were (6) _____ back to the station when it started to rain hard, and they didn't have any coats. Jim thought that his birthday was the biggest disaster ever, but then Peter started to laugh loudly and they agreed it was the funniest birthday ever.

2 Choose a title for this episode of *Friendly*.

a) The best day   b) The wrong map   c) What a disaster!

3 Find the one that doesn't belong.

1 across   past   (museum)   behind
   Museum because it's a building.
   _____

2 hotel   cab   restaurant   theater
   _____
   _____

3 stadium   left   between   right
   _____
   _____

4 lightning   rain   snow   tsunami
   _____
   _____

5 sailed   ran   flew   help
   _____
   _____

6 February   Thursday   April   October
   _____
   _____

4 Complete the sentences. Count and write the letters.

1 This is smaller than a road. It's a _street_____ . `6`

2 The lightning _____ their boat. ☐

3 The opposite of "inside" is _____ . ☐

4 The tenth month is _____ . ☐

5 There was a forest _____ last summer. It burned everything. ☐

6 The place where we go to catch a plane is an _____ . ☐

7 Cloud on the ground is called _____ . ☐

8 The month that comes before September is _____ . ☐

9 There's a _____ when there's heavy rain and a strong wind. ☐

10 We go to a _____ to see old books and paintings. ☐

11 We use a _____ to help us find our way. ☐

12 The point where two streets meet is a _____ . ☐

13 We need a _____ to walk over a river. ☐

14 The first month is _____ . ☐

5 Now complete the crossword puzzle. Write the message.

1	2	3	4	4	2	1		5	6	4	5	7	
s						s							!

6 Quiz time!

1 What's the name of the busiest airport in the world? _The busiest airport is_____
----

2 When was Mohenjo-Daro built?
----

3 What was Dan listening to on the boat?
----

4 What happened on May 6, 1937?
----

5 What does the Richter scale measure?
----

7 Write questions for your quiz in your notebook.

45

5 Material things

LOOK again | **Made of**

We use *made of* to describe materials.

Affirmative	Negative (n't = not)	Question
It's **made of** chocolate.	It isn't **made of** paper.	Is it **made of** sugar?
They're **made of** stone.	They aren't **made of** wood.	Are they **made of** leaves?

1 Match the words with the pictures.

grass	leaves	paper	~~bone~~
stone	brick		

1

2

3

bone _____ _____ _____

4

5

6

_____ _____ _____

2 Read and order the words.

1 made / This / is / jacket / fur. / of
   This jacket is made of fur.
2 isn't / skirt / That / made / chocolate. / of
   _____
3 your / of? / sweater / made / What's
   _____
4 T-shirt / your / Is / of / made / fur?
   _____
5 made / of / their / shoes / Are / wood?
   _____
6 paper. / clothes / made / are / of / His
   _____

3 Answer the questions.
What are they made of?

 1 *They're made of chocolate.* _____

 2 _____

 3 _____

 4 _____

 5 _____

 6 _____

4 Correct the sentences.

1 My hats is made of fur.

2 The spider has made of paper.

3 The cupcakes isn't made of chocolate.

4 Is his jacket made off rubber?

5 Are their houses mades of stone?

6 My candy are made of sugar.

5 Write the correct sentences.

Our house	made	of paper.
The boat is	is made	of rubber.
My book's	are made	of stone.
Their tires	made of	wood.

1 _____

2 _____

3 _____

4 _____

6 Read, look, and label the picture.

My house is made of trees, and it has grass on the roof. Grass is really good because it's very green. The house stays hot in the winter and cold in the summer. When it snows, I can ski on it!
The door is made of wood. The windows are made of water bottles. When it rains, the water from the roof goes into the window bottles. I use it to water my plants. There are leaves over the balcony. I can sit under these when it's sunny.

1 house made of trees

2 _____

    _____

3 _____

4 _____

5 _____

    _____

7 Read and complete the text.

bottles	bridges	thousand	~~materials~~	stone	gold

The Romans were the first people to use a lot of different
(1) materials _____ , both for building and in their everyday life. They were very good at making things from a lot of different metals, including
(2) _____ and silver.

    They made a lot of things with glass, like (3) _____ and glasses for drinking.

    The Romans made houses from wood, (4) _____ , and concrete. They also built 50,000 kilometers of roads and were the first people to be really good at making
(5) _____ . The first bridge with a name was the Pons Fabricius, made of stone. They built it over the River Tiber in Rome in 62 B.C., and it is there today, two
(6) _____ years later.

8 Choose words from the box to label the pictures.

| metal | silver | plastic | wood | ~~glass~~ | card | paper | wool | gold |

glass_____   _____   _____   _____   _____   _____

9 Find and write eight materials.

p	a	p	e	r	y	w	u	a	p
l	s	c	o	s	i	l	v	e	r
a	k	t	a	m	a	t	l	c	b
s	a	o	d	t	f	e	q	o	w
t	w	t	n	f	d	a	i	l	o
i	g	o	l	d	u	a	h	t	o
c	n	m	o	v	m	e	t	a	l
d	c	a	r	d	b	o	a	r	d

1 g o l d

2 s _____

3 p _____

4 w ____ d

5 c _____

6 p _____

7 m _____

8 w ____ l

10 Write the words.

1 A man-made material. We make it from oil. _plastic_____

2 An expensive white metal. _____

3 Animal hair. _____

4 Windows are made of this. It can break easily.

_____

5 We get this material from sheep. _____

11 Look at the letters on the clock and write the words.

1 It's twenty-five after twelve.
   gold_____

2 It's ten to three.
   _____

3 It's twenty-five to one.
   _____

4 It's half past four.
   _____

5 It's a quarter to eleven.
   _____

6 It's twenty to two.
   _____

ld
ver
at
wo
rd
sil
od
ca
tal
co
go
me

12 Read. Change one letter to write a new word.

face	Part of our body, on the front of our head.
race	A competition to see who's the fastest.
	Something we eat.
	Good, kind.
	A number between eight and ten.
	My things, something I have.
	A straight mark on a page or drawing.
	The opposite of *don't like*.
	Where do you … ?
	The opposite of *hate*.
	We do this with our body when we dance.
	Gold is … expensive than silver.
	The past of *wear*.
	The opposite of *play*.
	Part of a sentence.
	We get this material from trees.
	We get this material from sheep.
pool	Somewhere we can go to swim.

13 Now write the clues for this puzzle.

well	The opposite of "badly."
wall	
ball	
tall	
talk	
walk	

14 Find 8 mistakes in the text.

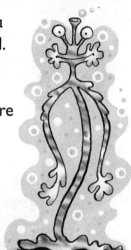

Glook's from a different world. He's doing a project about Earth, and there are a lot of mistakes. Can you help him correct his homework?

People on Earth use things that are made of different materials. Plastic, wood, and (dictionaries) are all different materials. Bottles are made of glass or paper. Tables and chairs can be made of fog, clouds, or metal. People on Earth like reading books, comic books, and volcanoes. These are made of cardboard and wool. Earth people get wool from parrots. I'm going to visit Earth next November. I want to get a nice big bracelet made of water. I can wear it when I go to parties.

15 Now write the text correctly.

People on Earth use things that are made of different materials. Plastic, wood, and cardboard are all different materials.

16 Match the rhyming words.

1	wool	a	where ____	6	box	f bricks ____
2	year	b	wood ____	7	six	g goes ____
3	stone	c	pull _1_	8	wear	h socks _6_
4	pear	d	here ____	9	nose	i ate ____
5	could	e	bone ____	10	great	j hair ____

17 **35 CD2** Listen, check, and say.

18 Read and match.

Write it right

Description of an object, how to use it, and why.
• This is a house.
• It's made of brick.
• I can use it to put my things in.
• I can play in it.
• It has a lot of windows because I like looking at the yard.

My dream house

1 My dream house is made   a food in it.

2 I can use it   b I like playing soccer.

3 I can cook my favorite   c of stone.   `1`

4 It has a big yard because   d so I can run around them.

5 There aren't any spiders in my house   e to sleep in.

6 There are ten rooms   f because I'm afraid of them.

19 Write about your dream house.

My dream house _____
My dream house is made of _____
_____
_____
_____
_____
_____
_____

20 Read and answer.

1 What was Brutus carrying in his backpack? <u>the Baloney Stone</u>
2 What's the inside of Brutus's backpack made of? _____
3 What did Brutus push? _____
4 Why's it dangerous to joke about Sirius? _____
5 What are the bowls made of? _____
6 What does Brutus want? _____

21 Read and order the text.

| in his backpack, but the Baloney Stone's safe ☐ |

| because the inside's made of plastic. Diggory ☐ |

| Brutus is carrying the computer [1] |

| the instructions. Brutus pushes the picture ☐ |

| Cleopatra's treasure from her underwater palace. ☐ |

| of the snake, and a secret door opens. They ☐ |

| find a lot of treasure behind the wall. It's ☐ |

| understands the writing on the wall and reads ☐ |

? Do you remember?

1 Trees are made of <u>wood</u> .
2 Scarves are made of _____ .
3 Gold and silver are precious _____ .
4 My friend is afraid _____ spiders.
5 A word that rhymes with "gold" is "_____."
6 Two words that rhyme with "great" are "_____" and "_____."

Can do   I can talk about materials.
              I can talk about what things are made of.
              I can write a description of a dream house.

Science   Recycling plastic

1 Look at the recycling facts. Read and write "true" or "false."

> Recycling can't take the colors from plastics, so we can't use them for transparent containers.

> When you put plastic bottles in recycling bins, both public and your own, always take the bottle cap off. If you take the cap off, it is easier to make them smaller.

> Every year in the United Kingdom, supermarkets give out 17,500,000,000 plastic bags. That is more than 290 for every person in the U.K.

> A lot of things are made from recycled plastic. These include polyethylene bags to put in recycling bins, PVC floors and windows, video and CD boxes, furniture, and waterproof clothes.

1 Take the cap off bottles when you recycle them. _true_
2 We use recycled plastic for recycling bin bags. _____
3 Recycling takes the colors from the plastic. _____
4 In the United Kingdom, supermarkets give out 17.5 million plastic bags a year. _____
5 PVC windows can be made of recycled plastic. _____
6 Supermarkets give people 50 bags a year. _____

2 What should we do? Put the information in the chart.

> ~~Throw plastic toys away~~   Give toys to friends or playgroups
> Use plastic containers and bags again   Make containers into something else
> Throw plastic containers away   Use a bag if you don't need one
> Look for products made from recycled plastic   Use a lot of plastic

Things we should do	Things we shouldn't do
	Throw plastic toys away

3 Write about plastic things you use in your school and the changes you are going to make.

Plastic in my school

52

4 **Whose things are these?**

Listen and write a letter in each box. There is one example.

Sarah `E`   Robert ☐   Emma ☐   Richard ☐   Katy ☐   Michael ☐

A

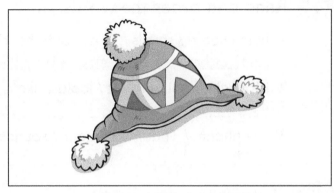

B

C

D

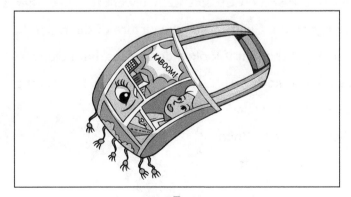

E

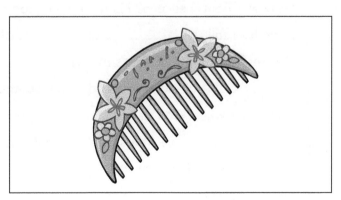

F

6 Senses

LOOK again | **What ... like?**

We use verb + *like* to describe things.

Affirmative	Negative (n't = not)	Question
It **looks like** a ball.	It **doesn't sound like** a car.	**What** does it **feel like**?
It **smells like** a lemon.	It **doesn't taste like** chocolate.	**What** does it **look like**?

1 Read and order the words.

1 blue cheese / smells / That / old / horrible.
   ~~That old blue cheese smells horrible.~~

2 it's / rain. / going to / It / looks / like
   ----

3 cell phone. / That / like / your / sounds
   ----

4 like? / does / this / toy mouse / What / feel
   ----

5 Her / cake / coffee. / tastes / like
   ----

6 look / like? / What / my picture / does
   ----

2 Correct the sentences.

1 Your cell phone sound ˢ˄ like a radio.

2 My sweater doesn't feels like fur.

3 That pen look likes a banana.

4 This cookie don't taste like chocolate.

5 What does that cheese smells like?

6 I doesn't look like my dad.

3 Read and complete the email.

| hear | ~~Saturday~~ | feel | exciting | felt | quickly | shouting |

Hi Frank,

How was your weekend? I had a really good one because on (1) _Saturday_ we went to a new theme park. It's really (2) ------------ and has a lot of things to do. Can you see the picture of the roller coaster? It's amazing! That's me (3) ------------ loudly. I thought it looked dangerous, but I didn't (4) ------------ afraid. It sounded very loud, though – I couldn't (5) ------------ anything. I also went on a ferris wheel. You sit in a chair and it goes around and around very (6) ------------ . At first I felt excited, but then I felt sick. When I got off, I didn't feel very well. I (7) ------------ sick. But I liked it.

Let's speak soon.

Richard

4 How do they look? Write the answers.

1 <u>She looks pleased.</u>
2 _____
3 _____
4 _____
5 _____
6 _____

5 Read. What are they?

1 It looks like an apple, but it isn't round. It's green and yellow. What is it? <u>a pear</u>

2 It looks like a bean, but it isn't. It's green, small, and round. What is it? _____

3 It's a fruit, and it tastes like a lime, but it isn't green. It's yellow. What is it? _____

4 It's a hot drink. Some people have it with sugar and milk. It sometimes looks like coffee, but it doesn't taste like coffee. What is it? _____

5 They sometimes taste like burgers. They are long and thin. What are they? _____

6 This sounds like a lion, but it isn't. It has orange fur and black stripes.
What is it? _____

6 Senses quiz. Read and answer.

1 Which part of the body do we use to taste? <u>Our tongue.</u>
2 Which part of the body do we use to smell? _____
3 Which parts of the body do we use to see? _____
4 Which parts of the body do we use to hear? _____
5 Which parts of the body can we use to touch things? _____
6 What are your favorite sounds? _____
7 What smells make you hungry? _____
8 Which of your senses do you think is the strongest? _____

7 Choose words from the box to label the pictures.

| flour | knife | salt | fork | ~~pepper~~ | spoon | plate | pizza |

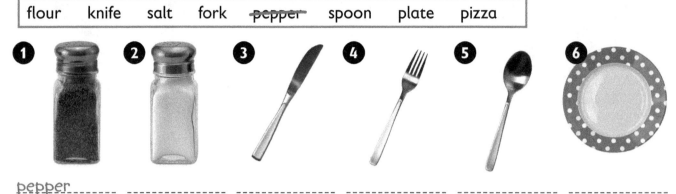

1 **2** **3** **4** **5** **6**

pepper _____ _____ _____ _____ _____ _____

8 Look and find the words.

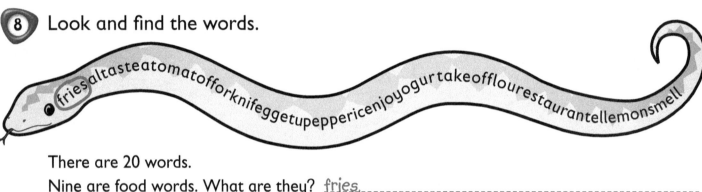

friesaltasteatomatofforknifeggetuppericenjoyogurtakeoffflourestaurantellemonsmell

There are 20 words.

Nine are food words. What are they? fries_____

_____

Seven are verbs (two of the verbs have two words). What are they? _____

_____

Two are things we eat with. What are they? _____

One is a preposition. What is it? _____

One is somewhere we go to eat. What is it? _____

9 Read and write the answers in the puzzle.

1 We put this on our food. It's black or white. pepper_____

2 We use this with a knife when we eat. _____

3 We use this in cooking. It's white. We get it
   from the ocean or the ground. _____

4 Famous Italian food. _____

5 We put our food on this when we
   eat. _____

6 Bread is made of this. _____

7 We use this to cut meat. _____

8 We use this to eat ice cream. _____

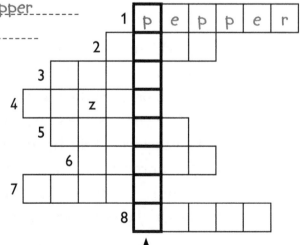

What's the mystery vegetable? _____

10 Read and complete the text.

900	meters	cook	meal	cheese	largest	flour
made	Italy	~~people~~	pizzas	top	taste	

ITALY

● Naples

The (1) people_____ from Naples (Napoli) in (2) _____ were the first to make (3) _____ . Their pizzas are (4) _____ of a bread base, with (5) _____ , tomato, and olives on top. Pizzas are people's favorite (6) _____ all over the world, not only in Italy, because they (7) _____ delicious. Some pizzas can have extra things on (8) _____ . They can have thicker bases, and sometimes the (9) _____ can fold the pizza in half and fill it with more cheese and things. They cook pizzas in an oven.

The (10) _____ pizza ever made was in South Africa in 1990. It was enormous! It was 37.4 (11) _____ across and was made with 500 kg of (12) _____ , 800 kg of cheese, and (13) _____ kg of tomatoes. Amazing!

11 Read and order the text.

	shows. When his family came home, it looked like the kitchen was on
	were out. He decided to cook sausages and potatoes. He turned on the
1	Tom's 14. Last Saturday he decided to make lunch for his family while they
	into the hot water. He did this because sugar looks like salt and he didn't read
6	the label on the box. Then he went into the living room to watch TV while he
	to turn on the clock. Then he started to cook the potatoes, but he put sugar
	was waiting for the food to cook and started to watch one of his favorite
9	fire. When they opened the oven, the sausages looked small and black. The
	potatoes were OK, but they tasted sweet. Tom's mom said he invented sweet potatoes!
	oven, and when it felt hot, he put the sausages inside, but he forgot

12 Write the words in the columns.

~~Daisy~~	~~Lucy~~	scarf	caps	amazing	dangerous
words	animals	center	cheese	smell	potatoes

s (plant<u>s</u>)	z (leg<u>s</u>)
<u>Lucy</u>	<u>Daisy</u>

13 🎵11 CD3 Listen, check, and say.

14 Read this diamante poem and answer the questions.

Summer
Hot,   dry
Playing, swimming, reading
Sun,   beach,   snow,   wind
Studying, sleeping, raining
Cold,   wet
Winter

Poems
Diamante poems always have seven lines and a specific number of words per line, in this order: one, two, three, four, three, two, one. They use the same kinds of words, and they are always in two halves.

Write it right

1 What's it about? <u>It's about summer and</u>

2 How does it make you feel?

15 Look at the poem again and complete the chart.

Line 1. 1 word   noun
Line 2. __ words   _____
Line 3. __ words   action verbs
Line 4. __ words   _____
Line 5. __ words   _____
Line 6. __ words   _____
Line 7. __ word   _____

16 Write your diamante poem.

17 Read and answer.

1 Where does Brutus fall? <u>He falls into a snake bowl.</u>
2 What's inside the snake bowl?
----
3 What does Diggory use to get Brutus out?
----
4 Who has the Baloney Stone now? -------------------------
5 What is the dog? -------------------------------------
6 Who does Brutus push into the snake bowl?
----

18 Correct the sentences.

1 At first, Brutus thought that the animals felt like a mouse.
<u>At first, Brutus thought that the animals felt like a spider.</u>
2 The dangerous ancient trap is called a snake plate.
----
3 Brutus loves spiders.
----
4 The snake didn't wake up.
----
5 Diggory used his scarf to help Brutus out of the snake bowl.
----
6 Brutus thought the dog was the window.

? **Do you remember?**

1 A lemon sometimes <u>looks</u> like a lime.
2 Pizza doesn't smell ----------------- spaghetti.
3 You need a spoon and a ----------------- to mix salad.
4 You need an ----------------- to cook pizza.
5 Two words that end with "s" (as in "plant<u>s</u>") are -----------------
and ----------------- .
6 A diamante poem has ----------------- lines.

Can do   I can talk about the five senses.
               I can plan a party.
               I can write a poem.

Art | Optical illusions

1 Read the text. What does it say? Write it correctly.

Cna yuo undretsnad waht tihs snetnece syas? Teh ltteres aer mexid up, so wehn yuo look at ti, it si dfificult ot undretsnad. Bceause yruo brian is vrey smtar, ti cna reda it.

Can _____

_____

_____

2 Look at the pictures. What can you see?

a

b

e

c

d

1 Can you read any words in a and b? _____

2 What are they? _____ _____ _____

3 Which line looks longer, c or d? _____

4 Now measure the two lines. What do you find out? _____

5 Which animal does it look like in e? _____

6 Now turn the picture around. Can you see a different animal? What is it? _____

3 Make your optical illusion.

• Color the squares: black–white– black–white …

• Don't color the gray lines.

What can you see? _____

_____

_____

4 Write about your favorite optical illusion.

My favorite optical illusion

5 **Look at the picture and read the story. Write some words to complete the sentences about the story. You can use 1, 2, 3, or 4 words.**

Helen is twelve, and she has a brother named William, who's six. Last Saturday Helen's dad took them to an art museum in the city center. They were very pleased. There was a show of modern art by a famous artist, and the museum was full of people. Helen was standing in front of a painting, looking at it, when William said, "This looks like a really big pizza with small tomatoes and olives on it."

Helen said, "You don't understand modern art, William. This is a great painting that shows us that life is beautiful, but difficult." Helen's dad laughed and said, "I think William understands modern art better than you, Helen. Look!" Helen's dad pointed, and Helen saw the title of the painting. It was called "Pizza with tomatoes and olives."

Example

Helen's brother is six .... years old.

Questions

1   Helen has .... named William.
2   Last Saturday Helen and William .... art museum with their father.
3   The show was by a famous artist, and there were a lot of .... at the museum.
4   One painting .... like a really big pizza.
5   Helen's dad read the title of the ....

Review Units  5 and 6

1 Read the story. Choose words from the box to complete the sentences.

pizza	flour	sounded	plastic	like	felt	were	~~competition~~	touch
movie	made							

Friendly

Last November Sue won an important art (1) _competition_ for her painting *Modern Girl*, which she said looked (2) _____ Jenny. The prize was a meal for two in Luigi's, the town's best Italian restaurant.

Sue invited Jenny to have lunch with her. Jenny felt very pleased. She bought a new dress that was (3) _____ of bright yellow wool. She wore it with a big brown (4) _____ belt and a dark brown jacket. She looked like a "Modern Girl," and she (5) _____ like a movie star. The two friends felt hungry when they arrived at the restaurant. The waiter put their (6) _____ on the table, and they agreed it smelled like the best in the world. When they were eating it, they said it tasted like nothing on Earth – it was delicious. After the pizza, Luigi came out of the kitchen and carefully put the second course on the table. It was his most famous dessert, Banana and Chocolate Surprise. Sue and Jenny felt very surprised. It looked just like Jenny's clothes!

2 Choose a title for this episode of *Friendly*.

a) The cook's famous clothes   b) A sweet dress   c) Jenny looks like a pear

3 Find the one that doesn't belong.

1 silver   metal   gold   (plastic)
   Plastic isn't a metal. _____

2 salt   olives   wool   pepper
   _____

3 eyes   feel   taste   smell
   _____

4 spoon   bracelet   knife   fork
   _____

5 wool   hair   stone   fur
   _____

6 wood   paper   cardboard   glass
   _____

Complete the sentences. Count and write the letters.

1 Her cell phone _sounds_ _ _ _ _ _ _ like a baby laughing.

2 We have five senses. They are sight, hearing, touch, smell, and _ _ _ _ _ _ _ _ _ _ _ _ _ _ .

3 We use a _ _ _ _ _ _ _ _ _ _ _ _ _ to cut meat.

4 _ _ _ _ _ _ _ _ _ _ _ _ _ is a material we get from sheep.

5 The opposite of "strong" is _ _ _ _ _ _ _ _ _ _ _ _ _ .

6 What does that cloud look _ _ _ _ _ _ _ _ _ _ _ _ _ ?

7 We hear with our _ _ _ _ _ _ _ _ _ _ _ _ _ .

8 We use a _ _ _ _ _ _ _ _ _ _ _ _ _ to eat soup.

9 _ _ _ _ _ _ _ _ _ _ _ _ _ is an expensive white metal.

10 Knives and forks can be made of metal or _ _ _ _ _ _ _ _ _ _ _ _ _ .

11 _ _ _ _ _ _ _ _ _ _ _ _ _ is a material we get from trees.

12 What's your bracelet _ _ _ _ _ _ _ _ _ _ _ _ _ of? Metal.

13 We feel _ _ _ _ _ _ _ _ _ _ _ _ _ if we don't drink.

14 We serve food on a _ _ _ _ _ _ _ _ _ _ _ _ _ .

6

5 **Now complete the crossword puzzle. Write the message.**

Crossword grid with letters: s, o, ³u, n, d, s, e, p, ⁵d, and numbers 2, 10, 9, 1, 6, 8, 7, 4

Message boxes:
1	2	3	4	5	1
		U			

6	7	8	9		10	3	4
					U			!

6 **Quiz time!**

1 What is Alex's spider made of?
   Alex's spider is made of fur _ _ _ _ _ _ _
   _

2 What is Arsenault's house made of?
   _

3 What is celluloid used for?
   _

4 What smells like Alex's socks?
   _

5 What does Luigi's Italian restaurant make? _ _ _ _ _ _ _ _ _ _ _ _ _ _ _ _ _ _ _

6 What does the painting *Mae West* look like? _ _ _ _ _ _ _ _ _ _ _ _ _ _ _ _ _ _

7 **Write questions for your quiz in your notebook.**

7 Natural world

We use *should* to give and ask for help or advice.

Affirmative	Negative (n't = not)	Question
I **should take care of** the country.	You **shouldn't throw** garbage on the ground.	**Should** he **help** his mom in the yard?
She **should clean up** her room.	We **shouldn't forget** that we have only one world.	**Should** they **drive** a big car?

1 Read and match.

1 What should you wear if you take a long walk?	You should wear a coat and scarf.
2 What should you wear outdoors on a sunny day?	You should stop and look both ways.
3 What should you wear when it's very cold?	1 You should wear strong shoes.
4 Who should you ask if you get lost in a big city?	To protect your skin from the sun.
5 What should you do when you cross the road?	You should ask a police officer.
6 Why should you use sunblock?	You should wear a hat.

2 Think and write "should" or "shouldn't."

1 It's a sunny day, and Emma's at the beach. She _should_ wear a hat.
2 Michael has a headache. He _____ watch TV.
3 Betty has a terrible toothache. She _____ go to the dentist.
4 David wants to cross the road. He _____ stop and look both ways first.
5 Katy _____ eat chocolate because she has a stomachache.
6 Harry has an important exam tomorrow, so he _____ study this afternoon.

3 Correct the sentences.

1 We've should take care of the country. _We should take care of the country._
2 We should to walk on the paths. _____
3 We should drop our garbage. _____
4 We always should use garbage cans. _____
5 We shouldn't of play with animals in fields. _____
6 We's shouldn't drink water from rivers. _____

4 **Match the problems with the correct advice.**

Pamela's Problem Page

1.
Dear Pamela,
I saw my friend copying during an exam. What should I do?

2.
Dear Pamela,
I'm having real problems with math in school. What should I do?

3.
Dear Pamela,
My friends are going to go to the movies on Saturday, but my parents say I can't go. What should I do?

4.
Dear Pamela,
I want to have a dog for my birthday, but my mom and dad say I can't have one. What should I do?

5.
Dear Pamela,
I want to learn to climb, but I don't live close to the mountains. What should I do?

6.
Dear Pamela,
I don't like vegetables, but my mom says I have to eat carrots and peas every day. I hate dinnertime. What should I do?

a.
Why don't you talk to them and ask to go to see the movie another day? You should ask them to come with you.

b.
If you don't understand something, you should always talk to your teacher. She'll be pleased to help you.

c.
You should look on the Internet for a climbing club in your closest city. You can climb up special climbing walls.

d.
You should ask your mom if you can try a different vegetable every day until you find some that you like.

e.
It's important to remember that if your parents say no, they know why. Ask them to talk to you about it.

f.
You should talk to your friend and tell him or her not to do it again. If that doesn't work, then tell your teacher.

1 [f]   2 [ ]   3 [ ]   4 [ ]   5 [ ]   6 [ ]

5 **Think and write advice.**

1 Someone who's going to the beach on a hot day.
2 Someone who has a headache.
3 Someone who wants to learn English.
4 Someone who wants to try a new hobby.
5 Someone who wants to learn more about the past.
6 Someone who is always fighting with their brother.

1 | You should take a hat and sunblock. You shouldn't lie in the sun all day.

6 **Answer the questions.**

1 Do your friends talk to you when they have a problem? ____
2 Do you help your friends? ____
3 Do you think you should always keep secrets? ____
4 Who do you talk to when you have a problem? ____
5 What are the biggest problems for you and your friends? ____
6 When should you tell your teacher about a problem? ____

7 Choose words from the box to label the pictures.

> Lehmann's poison frog   Purple spotted butterfly   ~~Mountain zebra~~
> Siberian tiger   Nine-spotted ladybug beetle

Mountain _____ _____ _____ _____ _____
zebra _____ _____ _____ _____ _____

8 Unscramble and write the words.

1 sigwn	_wings_____	4 opst	_____	7 iatl	_____
2 erttflbyu	_____	5 pitser	_____	8 dboy	_____
3 tisnce	_____	6 ufr	_____	9 tbeele	_____

9 Now match the words with the definitions.

1 _beetle_____ This insect has two hard wings and two soft wings.
2 _____ The hair an animal has on its body.
3 _____ The parts of an insect or animal that it uses to fly.
4 _____ Lions, tigers, elephants, and mice all have one of these. It comes out of the back part of their bodies.
5 _____ The part of an animal or insect that has the arms and legs on it.
6 _____ An insect with two beautiful wings, six legs, and two antennae.
7 _____ A small animal with a body, six legs, and two eyes.
8 _____ A small colored circle on a different color.
9 _____ An area between two lines that is a different color.

10 Write the words in the chart.

> ~~through~~   ~~become~~   ~~funny~~   ~~spot~~   extinction   recycle   wing   into   appear
> extinct   spotted   over   across   explore   stripe   warm

adjectives	verbs	prepositions	nouns
_funny_____ _____	_become_____ _____	_through____ _____	_spot_____ _____
_____ _____	_____ _____	_____ _____	_____ _____

11 Match the pictures of endangered animals with the words.

1 Leatherback turtle [a]
2 Orangutan [ ]
3 White rhino [ ]
4 Iberian lynx [ ]
5 Whale [ ]
6 Giant panda [ ]
7 Bearded vulture [ ]
8 Bat [ ]

12 Now find out one fact about each of the endangered animals in Activity 11.

Leatherback turtles live in the Pacific Ocean.

13 Now make a quiz for your friends.

Endangered animals quiz
1 Where do leatherback turtles live?

14 Read and order the story.

	"What is your question?" the teacher asked.
	The old man said, "I don't know either. Here are your two dollars!"
1	One day a very smart teacher went to a small town in the country.
	The teacher was happy with the old man's idea because he was very smart.
	The teacher thought for a long time, but he didn't know the answer.
	"What animal has three heads, two wings, and one leg?" the old man asked.
	He was talking to the people there when an old man spoke to him: "I have a question for you. If you can't answer my question, you give me ten dollars. Then you ask me a question. If I can't answer it, I give you two dollars."
	After thinking for 30 minutes, he gave the old man his ten dollars and said, "I'm sorry. I don't know the answer. What is it?"

15 Write the opposites.

| white | ~~old~~ | long | past | cold | night | strong | last |

1 young and _old_
2 hot and _____
3 black and _____
4 day and _____

5 short and _____
6 weak and _____
7 present and _____
8 first and _____

16 [22 CD3] Listen, check, and say.

17 Read and number the parts of the letter.

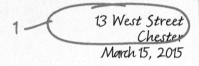

1 — 13 West Street
Chester
March 15, 2015

Dear Mrs. Smith,

I'm writing to ask you for information about recycling bins at our school.

In my class we think we should recycle all paper and bottles. There are some questions I'd like to ask. Can you bring some recycling bins to our school, please? Also, when can I come to talk to you?

Thank you very much.

Regards,
Emily Wood

Writing a letter
A polite letter should have:
1 Your address
2 Today's date
3 The name of the person you're writing to
4 The reason you're writing
5 An end
6 Your name

Write it right

18 Now write a letter to Mrs. Green about recycling. Ask her for information about the recycling bins.

_____
_____
_____

Dear Mrs. Green,
_____
_____
_____
_____
_____
_____
_____

19 Read and answer.

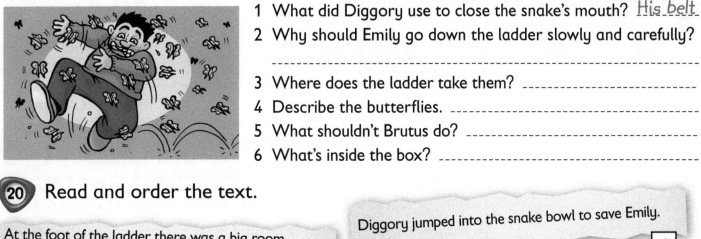

1 What did Diggory use to close the snake's mouth? <u>His belt</u>

2 Why should Emily go down the ladder slowly and carefully?
----

3 Where does the ladder take them? --------------------------

4 Describe the butterflies. ------------------------------------

5 What shouldn't Brutus do? ---------------------------------

6 What's inside the box? --------------------------------------

20 Read and order the text.

At the foot of the ladder there was a big room full of butterflies. ☐

Thousands of butterflies flew off the walls to protect their young. ☐

There was a ladder under the door. They climbed slowly and carefully down it. ☐

Then he put his belt round the snake's mouth so it couldn't bite them. ☐

Diggory jumped into the snake bowl to save Emily. 1

The box was full of striped insects, so Brutus dropped it. ☐

Diggory knew how to get out. He opened a secret door. ☐

When Diggory and Emily were looking at the butterflies, Brutus opened a box. ☐

The room was the famous butterfly room of Queen Hetepheres. ☐

? Do you remember?

1 I have a problem. What <u>should</u> I do?

2 You ------------------ throw garbage on the floor. Put it in a garbage can.

3 The Lost Ladybug Project asks people to take ------------------ of these endangered beetles.

4 Two endangered animals that have ------------------ are tigers and zebras.

5 "Hot" and "------------------" are opposites.

6 You should write your ------------------ on the top right corner of a letter.

Can do I can describe insects and animals.
I can talk about things we should or shouldn't do.
I can write a letter.

1 Read the fact sheet and complete the text.

Name	When it died	Where	Description	Interesting facts
Archaeopteryx	About 150 million years ago	Germany in Europe	Length – 30 cm long from beak to tail Wings – 0.5 m across Weight – 300–500 grams	The Archaeopteryx was the first animal to fly. It ate meat.

The (1) Archaeopteryx was a dinosaur that lived about a hundred and (2) _____ million years ago. It lived in (3) _____ in Europe. It was (4) _____ cm long and had (5) _____ that were 50 centimeters across. It weighed between (6) _____ hundred and five (7) _____ grams. The Archaeopteryx was the first (8) _____ to fly. Its favorite food was (9) _____ .

2 Now read and write about the Diplodocus.

Name	When it died	Where	Description	Interesting facts
Diplodocus	About 145–155 million years ago	There are a lot of Diplodocus bones in the Rocky Mountains in the U.S.A.	Length – 27 m long Height – 5 m tall Weight – 10–20 tons	The Diplodocus was enormous. It had an 8-meter-long neck and a 14-meter-long tail. Its head was not more than 60 cm long. Its front legs were shorter than its back legs, and all legs had feet like an elephant's. It was a herbivore and ate leaves from trees.

The Diplodocus was an enormous dinosaur that lived

Listen and draw lines. There is one example.

Betty   Harry   Richard   George

Katy   Holly   Sarah

8 World of sports

We use the *present perfect* to talk and write about things we did and do.

Affirmative	Negative (n't = not)	Question
I**'ve played** tennis.	You **haven't played** volleyball.	**Has** he **played** basketball?
She**'s been** skiing.	We **haven't been** swimming.	**Have** they **been** running?

1 Are these verbs regular or irregular? Write "R" or "I."

arrive _R_   lose _I_   believe ____   make ____   stop ____   play ____

meet ____   catch ____   jump ____   win ____   finish ____   wash ____

2 Make negative sentences.

1 I've sailed from England to Ireland.
I haven't sailed from England to Ireland.

2 She's won a prize.
_____

3 They've played basketball.
_____

4 He's climbed the highest mountain.
_____

5 You've won the game.
_____

6 We've made a kite.
_____

3 Match the pictures with the text.

It's the first time she's played badminton!

It's the first time he's won a prize. ☐ 1

I've never made a cake before. ☐

This is the first time you've worked in a restaurant, isn't it? ☐

Is this the first time they've washed the car? ☐

We've never been ice-skating before. ☐

4 Answer the questions.

1 What's the third letter in **heard**? _a_
2 What's the second letter in **climbed**? ____
3 What's the fifth letter in **stopped**? ____
4 What's the first letter in **healthy**? ____
5 What's the third letter in **skated**? ____
6 What's the first letter in **badminton**? ____
7 What's the sixth letter in **started**? ____
8 What's the first letter in **tennis**? ____

What's the word? _____

5 Now make your word puzzle.

1 What's the seventh letter in **basketball**?
2 What's the first letter in **appeared**?

6 Write the correct form of the verbs in the email.

Hi Joe,

I'm writing to tell you about the things I've
(1) _done_ (do) in the last month or two. We haven't
(2) _____ (talk) for two months. I'm sorry, but
I've been really busy. I've (3) _____ (study) a lot
because I have exams next week. I've finally
(4) _____ (finish) the book that you gave me for
my birthday. It was really interesting.

   Let me tell you what's (5) _____ (happen) at
the sports center. You know that I was on the field hockey
team, don't you? Well, I've (6) _____ (decide) to
change sports. I've (7) _____ (stop) playing field
hockey, and now I've (8) _____ (start) racing my
bike. It's very difficult, but I like it. I've (9) _____
(race) twice, and I finished fifth and ninth. Not bad, really.
Look at the picture. I'm in it!

Have you ever (10) _____ (win) a race?

Write soon!

7 Look at the pictures. Write the questions.

What have they done? _____

_____

_____ _____

_____ _____

_____ _____

_____ _____

8 Now answer the questions.

1 _They've arrived in Washington._
2 _____
3 _____
4 _____
5 _____
6 _____

9 Choose words from the box to label the pictures.

| golf | sledding | volleyball | track and field | ~~skiing~~ | snowboarding | cycling | tennis |

     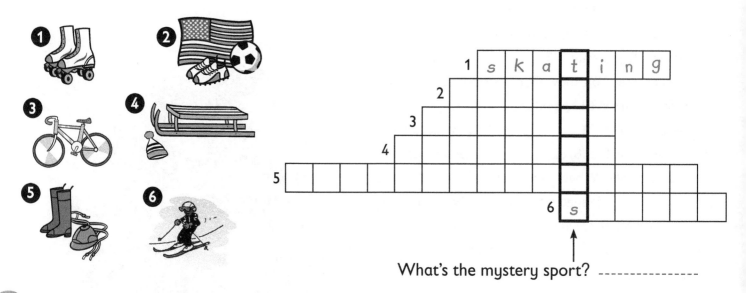

skiing _____ _____ _____ _____ _____ _____

10 Write the seasons.

1 This is the hottest season. summer_____

2 In this season all the new flowers start growing. _____

3 This is the season when trees lose their leaves. _____

4 This is the coldest season. This season comes after the fall. _____

11 Write the sports words in the chart.

| ~~soccer~~ | Ping-Pong | sailing | ice-skating | basketball | sledding |
| cycling | horseback riding | skiing | tennis | ice hockey | track and field |

winter sports	ball sports	other sports
_____	soccer_____	_____
_____	_____	_____
_____	_____	_____
_____	_____	_____

12 What are the sports? Write the words in the puzzle.

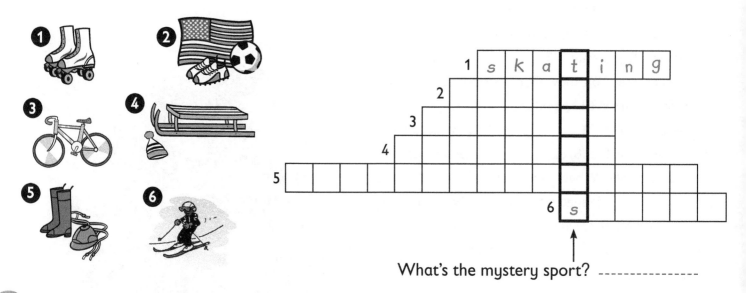

What's the mystery sport? _____

74

13 Write the sports.

| snowboarding | ~~Ping-Pong~~ | sailing | golf | basketball | waterskiing |

1 You play inside with a small ball, two bats, and a table. _Ping-Pong_

2 This is a team sport. Each team has five players. In this sport you can bounce, throw, and catch the big ball. _____

3 You do this sport on mountains when there is snow. You have to stand up to do it. _____

4 You do this sport on water. You need a boat. _____

5 You can do this in an ocean or a lake. You stand up and a boat pulls you. _____

6 This is not a team sport, and you have to play outside. The players hit a very small ball around a course with 18 holes. _____

14 Now write definitions for six more sports.

| 1 | You usually play this sport outside. You need a bicycle. |

15 Read and complete the chart.

Three friends live in houses next to each other on Ice Road, and they have made a snowman. Where does each friend live? What has each child brought to put on the snowman?

  Robert lives at number 3. He didn't bring a carrot for the snowman's nose. Sally brought a scarf for the snowman. Richard doesn't live next to Robert. One of the boys brought a hat for the snowman.

Name			Robert
House number			
Thing for the snowman			

16 Choose the story. Then draw your snowman in your notebook.

Last weekend it was very cold, and it snowed a lot. We went outside to play in the **park** / **forest** / **yard**. First we **played** / **jumped** / **sledded** in the snow. Then we decided to make a **big** / **small** / **tall** / **fat** / **funny** / **thin** snowman.

  When we finished making it, we gave it a **carrot** / **banana** / **pear** for a nose and some **leaves** / **rocks** / **stones** for a mouth. Then we put an old **brown** / **red** / **purple** hat on its head and a long **spotted** / **striped** scarf around its neck. The scarf was **blue and green** / **pink and purple** / **red and yellow**. Finally we put two **orange** / **gray** / **black** gloves on sticks and put them into its body. The gloves were made of **leather** / **wool** / **rubber**. Our snowman looked **happy** / **sad** / **surprised** / **angry** / **amazing**. We called it _____ .

17 Match the rhyming words.

1 wore   a through ____   7 laughed   g should ____
2 said   b bought ____   8 heard   h child ____
3 skated   c made ____   9 won   i belt ____
4 flew   d four _1_   10 felt   j craft _7_
5 played   e head ____   11 stood   k word ____
6 caught   f waited ____   12 smiled   l done ____

18 [34 CD3] Listen, check, and say.

19 Find and circle information about what, when, where, and why. Make four circles in total.

To: bill@kidsbox/.co.uk

Hi Bill,

what →

I'm writing you a quick email to tell you about the (soccer game) I went to on the weekend. My dad took me to see our town team in Springfield. The Springfield Flyers played against the K.B. Rovers. We love soccer! It was a great game. Both teams scored a goal in the first half. It was really exciting! Then, five minutes before the end of the game, the Springfield Flyers scored their second goal. I was really excited and threw my scarf up in the air. The wind caught it, and it fell onto a lady's head. I said sorry, but she didn't think it was funny. That wasn't surprising because she was a K.B. Rovers supporter!

Dad and I laughed about it when we got home.

C U soon!
Bye for now,
Dave

Emails
- An email to a friend is normally very friendly.
- You need to write your friend's email address in the box at the top.
- You don't need to write your address or the date.
- You can start your email saying "Hi" or "Hello."
- To make your email interesting, include information about what, when, where, and why.
- You can finish your email saying "All the best" or "Bye for now."

Write it right

20 Now write your email about something that happened on the weekend.

Hi _____ ,
I'm writing you a quick email _____
_____
_____
_____
_____
_____

21 Read and answer.

1 Why shouldn't Brutus open his mouth? <u>The butterflies are dangerous.</u>
2 Has Diggory ever used the new door? _____
3 Which sports did the ancient Egyptians invent? _____
4 Where did Diggory send the email from? _____
5 What does the Ancient Story of Sirius say? _____
_____

22 Who said it? Read and match.

1  **2**  **3**  **4**

a They've painted sports on these walls. `3`

b It's the first time anybody's used this door. ☐

c I've waited for this moment all my life. ☐

d Now what have you done? ☐

e I haven't touched anything. ☐

f You're the treasure now, Brutus! ☐

? Do you remember?

1 Have you ever <u>been</u> to Egypt?
2 He's _____ the race. Now he can celebrate!
3 They haven't _____ badminton before.
4 _____ is the season that comes after spring.
5 One word that rhymes with "said" is _____.
6 You can say "_____ for now" at the end of an email to a friend.

Can do
I can talk about things I have done.
I can talk about different sports.
I can write an email.

1 Choose words from the box to complete the text.

| soccer | countries | always | ~~four~~ | started | well | athletes | swimming |

There are Paralympic Games every (1) four_____ years. Paralympic Games are

(2) _____ in the same city as the full Olympic Games. They are for (3) _____

who have a disability. "Disability" means they have problems doing some things. Some athletes

can't see (4) _____ or can't see at all, and others can't walk. The Paralympic Games

(5) _____ in Rome in 1960, and in each Paralympics there are more (6) _____

and more athletes competing.

2 Invent a sport for the next Olympics.

Write your ideas on the mind map.

When?
_____

Name
_____

How many
people?
_____

My Olympic sport
_____

Equipment
_____
_____
_____

Rules
_____
_____
_____
_____

Where?
_____

Prize
_____

3 Now use the information in your mind map to write a letter to the Olympic
Committee telling them about your sport.

Dear Olympic Committee,
I'm writing to tell you about my new sport. I would like it to be in the
next Olympic Games. It's called

4 **Read the text. Choose the right words and write them on the lines.**

Winter sports

Example	Winter sports is what we call sports ..that................ people
1	do and play on snow and ice. .... sports are very
2	popular in countries where it is cold in .... winter.
3	One of the most popular sports is skiing. There ....
4	three kinds of .... at the Olympic Games today.
5	One is downhill skiing, where .... race down
6	a hill. In another kind, people .... through
	the countryside. They can race up to fifty kilometers.
7	The .... kind is ski jumping, which is very
8	.... Ice-skating, snowboarding, and sledding
9	are just some .... the other winter sports. At the
10	Winter Olympic Games there are .... than ten
	different sports.

Example	who	when	that
1	This	That	These
2	the	a	those
3	is	are	was
4	skied	skiing	skying
5	person	people	persons
6	racing	race	races
7	three	third	thirty
8	excited	excites	exciting
9	of	at	over
10	most	much	more

Review Units 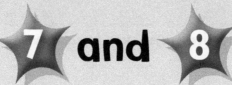 7 and 8

1 Read the story. Choose a word from the box. Write the correct word next to numbers 1–6.

| taking | was | ride | snowman | ~~ever~~ | were | done | skis | coming |
| sled | are |

Friendly

Have you (1) _ever_____ been skiing? This is what happened to Jim and Sally when they went last winter.

   Last January the five friends went skiing with the school. On the first day, Sue, Peter, and Jenny decided that it was too dangerous for them, so they chose a sled and found somewhere nice and quiet at the bottom of the mountain to (2) _____ on it.
Jim and Sally got their skis and went quickly to the ski lift that was taking the other skiers to the top of the mountain. It was Sally's first time on a ski lift, but Jim told her it was easy, and she felt really excited. They sat on the thin metal seat, holding the long piece of metal that was between them, and the lift started. When they (3) _____ going up the mountain, Sally fell off. She fell onto her face and stomach with her skis crossed behind her, and she couldn't move. The other skiers, who were coming up on the lift behind her, couldn't stop and fell off, too. Sally took her (4) _____ off to move away, but she dropped them, and they fell quickly down the mountain.

   Sue, Peter, and Jenny, who were sledding happily at the bottom of the mountain, suddenly saw Sally's skis coming, but they couldn't do anything, and the skis hit their (5) _____ . They all fell off into the snow.
On the second day, the friends decided to do something safer. They made a (6) _____!

2 Choose a title for this episode of *Friendly*.

a) Snow feels cold   b) Snowy disaster!   c) Summer holidays

3 Match the questions with the answers.

1	What can you catch, but not throw?		A watchdog.
2	Waiter! Waiter! What's this fly doing on my ice cream?		Because 7 ate 9.
3	Where do horses go when they feel sick?		I think it's skiing, sir.
4	What's worse than finding an insect in your apple?	1	A cold.
5	What goes "Tick tock woof tick tock woof"?		To a horspital.
6	Why was 10 afraid of 7?		Finding only half an insect in your apple.

4 Complete the sentences. Count and write the letters.

1 Snowboarding isn't easy. It's pretty difficult_____ . [9]

2 Have you _____ won a prize? No, never. [ ]

3 When a plant or animal species doesn't exist anymore, it's _____ . [ ]

4 He's _____ his homework, so now he can watch TV. [ ]

5 When something has spots, it's _____ . [ ]

6 What _____ they done? They've washed the car. [ ]

7 When we have a picnic, we _____ pick up our garbage. [ ]

8 The Diplodocus is an extinct _____ . [ ]

9 Animals that fly need two _____ . [ ]

10 He's the winner. He's _____ higher than the other jumpers. [ ]

11 The Olympic _____ is a sports competition that is every four years. [ ]

12 Zebras have black and white _____ on their fur. [ ]

13 Animal hair is called _____ . [ ]

14 You play _____ on grass, hitting a small ball into holes with a long stick. [ ]

5 Now complete the crossword puzzle. Write the message.

1	2	3	1		4	2	5	6
					f			

d i ⁴f f i c u l t

6 Quiz time!

1 What should people do with their garbage?
They should_____

2 What has two soft and two hard wings?
_____

3 Why did the dinosaurs become extinct?
_____

4 How many races has Alex won?
_____

5 When do people go skiing?
_____

6 Where were the 2012 Olympics?
_____

7 Write questions for your quiz in your notebook.

1 Read and choose the answer.

How good a student are you?

1 How often do you have breakfast before you go to school?

a never   b sometimes   c always

2 What time do you go to bed on school days?

a after 11 o'clock
b at about ten o'clock
c before ten o'clock

3 When do you prepare your school bag?

a before I go to bed
b I don't prepare it
c before I leave the house

4 How often do you talk to your friends during class?

a never   b sometimes   c always

5 Is it funny to take your friend's pencil case during the lesson?

a Yes   b I don't know   c No

6 When do you normally arrive for your classes?

a when you want to
b after the class starts
c before the class starts

2 Write a class contract.

1 We must arrive on time.
2 ....
3 ....
4 ....
5 ....
6 When we do all these things correctly, we can:
   • ....
   • ....

Class Contract

People who help us

 1 Read and order the text.

	his car. Firefighters had to cut the car door
	accident. The police officers drove Harry
	much better. He's going to leave the
	had a bad car accident. His car hit a
	the hospital a team of doctors and
	officers called the hospital and
	Harry's life. Now, two weeks later, Harry is
	truck, and he couldn't get out of
	told the nurses about Harry and his
	to help stop the traffic. At
	to the hospital with the ambulance
	nurses worked together to save
1	Last week William's dad, Harry,
	hospital and go home to his family.
	and pull Harry out. Police

2 Write a letter to thank the firefighters.

Imagine that you are William. Write a letter to say thank you to the firefighters, police officers, and doctors who saved your dad's life. Use these words to help you.

two weeks ago   operate   great job   accident   help   save life
now better   Best wishes

Dear Superheroes,

Tell the truth but don't hurt

1 Read and answer the questions.

It is always important to tell the truth. But there are some times in life when it's not the best thing to do. These times are usually when we don't want to hurt other people's feelings. The truth can sometimes make other people feel bad or unhappy. Not telling the truth is called "telling a lie." When we do this because we don't want to hurt someone, it's called "telling a little white lie" and it's OK.

1 How can telling the truth sometimes make people feel? ----------------------------------
2 Why do we tell little white lies? --
3 Do you ever tell little white lies? ---
4 When was the last time you told a little white lie? ------------------------------------

2 Imagine a situation and write about telling a little white lie.

It was ...

Value your friendships

1 Write the sentences and questions.

1 I / help / can / my / friend? / How   <u>How can I help my friend?</u>

2 tell / didn't / I / the / truth --

3 speak / should / Who / he / to? --

4 friend / best / in / cheats / My / exams --

5 really / big / made / I've / mistake / a --

6 do? / should / I / What --

2 Read the letter and answer the questions.

Dear Betty and Robert,

I'm worried about my friend, Peter. He has some new friends in school, and they like doing bad things. Peter really wants to be part of their group. They told him to go to the shopping mall and steal some things. Peter doesn't feel that this is wrong. He has started to take little things from a small store close to where he lives. He says he's practising because there are a lot of cameras in the big mall. I told him that these boys aren't really his friends and that the police can catch him, but he doesn't want to listen and laughs at me. He thinks it's a joke. What should I do?

Yours,

Daisy

1 How can Daisy help Peter?   <u>She should</u> ---------------------------

2 Who can Daisy talk to? --

3 Should Daisy tell Peter's parents? --

4 Should Daisy tell a teacher? --

3 Write a reply to Daisy.

Grammar reference

1 Write the times.

1 `7:20` Jim got up at _twenty after seven_ .

2 `7:45` He took a shower at _____ .

3 `7:55` He got dressed at _____ .

4 `8:05` He ate his breakfast at _____ .

5 `8:25` He went to school at _____ .

6 `8:50` He arrived at school at _____ .

2 Read and write.

1 They're going to play tennis. (soccer) _No, they aren't. They're going to play soccer._

2 She's going to eat some cheese. (meat) _____

3 He's going to have lunch in school. (home) _____

4 We're going to get up early. (late) _____

5 I'm going to buy a new CD. (comic book) _____

6 It's going to rain. (snow) _____

3 Read and choose the right words.

1 She rode her bike **down** / **left** the road.

2 They drove **past** / **right** the school.

3 He took the fourth street on the **straight ahead** / **right**.

4 The museum was **across** / **corner** the street.

5 I turned **straight ahead** / **left** at the post office.

6 The bus stopped at the **corner** / **across**.

4 Read and order the words.

1 (his) (George wasn't) (homework.) (doing)

   George wasn't doing his homework.

2 (in the) (Sarah skiing) (mountains?) (Was)

   _____

3 (I) (bath.) (taking a) (wasn't)

   _____

4 (to an) (sailing) (island.) (David was)

----

5 (Emma and Harry) (the park.) (through) (were running)

----

6 (the bus stop?) (Were) (waiting at) (you)

----

5 Answer the questions.

1 What are these bowls made of? (relvis)   *They're made of silver.* _____
2 What's this comic book made of? (reppa)   _____
3 What are his shoes made of? (threale)   _____
4 What's her scarf made of? (lowo)   _____
5 What are windows made of? (sagls)   _____
6 What's that watch made of? (logd)   _____

6 Complete the sentences.   (like   cheese   It   feel   ~~tired~~)

1 She looked *tired* _____ .   4 We didn't _____ sad.
2 They tasted _____ mangoes.   5 _____ doesn't sound very nice.
3 It smelled like _____ .

7 Read and write "Yes, you should." or "No, you shouldn't."

1 Should you leave your garbage on the ground?   *No, you shouldn't.* _____
2 Should you play your music very loudly?   _____
3 Should you use sunblock when you go to the beach?   _____
4 Should you play with animals in fields?   _____
5 Should you wear strong shoes when you walk in the mountains?   _____
6 Should you drink water from a river?   _____

8 Write questions and answers.

1 she / ever / climb / mountain? (✓) *Has she ever climbed a mountain? Yes, she has.*
2 they / ever / enter / competition? (✗) _____ _____
3 he / ever / play / Ping-Pong? (✗) _____ _____
4 they / ever / make / snowman? (✓) _____ _____
5 you / ever / see / the Olympics? (✗) _____ _____

Irregular verbs

Infinitive	Past tense	Past participle
be	was/were	been
be called	was/were called	been called
be going to	was/were going to	been going to
begin	began	begun
break	broke	broken
bring	brought	brought
buy	bought	bought
can	could	could
catch	caught	caught
choose	chose	chosen
come	came	come
cut	cut	cut
do	did	done
draw	drew	drawn
drink	drank	drunk
drive	drove	driven
dry	dried	dried
eat	ate	eaten
fall	fell	fallen
fall over	fell over	fallen over
feel	felt	felt
find	found	found
find out	found out	found out
fly	flew	flown
forget	forgot	forgotten
get	got	gotten
get (un)dressed	got (un)dressed	gotten (un)dressed
get (up/on/off)	got (up/on/off)	gotten (up/on/off)
get to	got to	gotten to
give	gave	given
go	went	gone
go out	went out	gone out
go shopping	went shopping	gone shopping
grow	grew	grown
have	had	had
have to	had to	had to
hear	heard	heard
hide	hid	hidden
hit	hit	hit
hold	held	held
hurt	hurt	hurt

Infinitive	Past tense	Past participle
keep	kept	kept
know	knew	known
leave	left	left
let	let	let
lie down	lay down	lain down
lose	lost	lost
make	made	made
make sure	made sure	made sure
mean	meant	meant
meet	met	met
must	had to	had to
put	put	put
put on	put on	put on
read	read	read
ride	rode	ridden
run	ran	run
say	said	said
see	saw	seen
sell	sold	sold
send	sent	sent
sing	sang	sung
sit	sat	sat
sleep	slept	slept
speak	spoke	spoken
spend	spent	spent
stand	stood	stood
steal	stole	stolen
swim	swam	swum
swing	swung	swung
take	took	taken
take a picture	took a picture	taken a picture
take off	took off	taken off
teach	taught	taught
tell	told	told
think	thought	thought
throw	threw	thrown
understand	understood	understood
wake up	woke up	woken up
wear	wore	worn
win	won	won
write	wrote	written

My languages

This portfolio is to help you learn English. You can add more pages about learning English or other languages.

All languages are fantastic!

What languages do you know?

Write the languages you know. Check (✓) the boxes.

Language: _____

I speak this language:

at home ☐   in school ☐   on the street ☐   on vacation ☐

I meet people who speak this language: often ☐   sometimes ☐

I do these things in this language:

talk with my friends ☐   read books ☐   read magazines ☐

watch TV shows ☐   watch movies ☐   write messages/emails ☐

Language: _____

I speak this language:

at home ☐   in school ☐   on the street ☐   on vacation ☐

I meet people who speak this language: often ☐   sometimes ☐

I do these things in this language:

talk with my friends ☐   read books ☐   read magazines ☐

watch TV shows ☐   watch movies ☐   write messages/emails ☐

Language: _____

I speak this language:

at home ☐   in school ☐   on the street ☐   on vacation ☐

I meet people who speak this language: often ☐   sometimes ☐

I do these things in this language:

talk with my friends ☐   read books ☐   read magazines ☐

watch TV shows ☐   watch movies ☐   write messages/emails ☐

Language Portfolio language skills: My progress

What can you do in English in the classroom?   Date: _____

Skill	What I can do	I can do it easily: ✓✓ I can do it: ✓ I want more practice: !!
Listening	I can understand: • when my teacher asks me to do things in the classroom (e.g., raise my hand, be quiet, close the door, open my book, clean up, etc.) • when my teacher tells me to do an activity or shows me how to play a game (e.g., write the numbers in the boxes, order the words to make sentences, etc.) • the instructions and listening activities on the *Kid's Box* CD	
Reading	I can understand English words and sentences: • when my teacher writes on the board • in my Student's Book and Workbook	
Speaking	Talking with another person, I can: • tell my partner about some things I like and don't like • ask my teacher for things (e.g., a pencil or paper, to go to the bathroom, etc.) • raise my hand and answer the questions my teacher asks me	
	Talking to the class, I can: • talk about a project we did in class	
Writing	I can write: • a birthday, Christmas, or Easter card and invite my friend to a party • about me, my family, and where I live	

Teacher's comments: _____

I can ... Units 1 and 2

| I can do it easily: ✓✓ |
| I can do it: ✓ |
| I want more practice: !! |

1  Listening. I can understand when someone tells me the time.

What time is it, please?

It's a quarter after eleven.

2 Speaking. I can say what TV shows I like and don't like. I can say why.

I like documentaries. They're really interesting!

I don't like watching the weather. It's boring!

3  Reading. I can understand the Diggory Bones comic book in the *Kid's Box* Student's Book.

Good work!

4 Writing. I can write about my plans for next week (with *going to*).

Next week
On Monday after school I'm going
to English class. On Tuesday ...

1	
2	
3	
4	

I can ...   Units 3 and 4

I can do it easily: ✓✓ I can do it: ✓ I want more practice: ‼

1 🎧 Listening. I can understand directions to get to a place on a map (turn right / turn left / go straight ahead ...).

Where's the movie theater, please?

Go straight ahead. Turn right ...

1

2 💬 Speaking. I can find the differences between two pictures and say what they are.

In the first picture there's a green bus, but in the second there's a red bus.

2

3 🔍 Reading. I can read about the first cities and answer the questions.

3

4 ✏️ Writing. I can write about what happened to me last week in my diary.

On Saturday I went to the park to
play with my friends. We ...

4

I can ... Units 5 and 6

	I can do it easily: ✓✓ I can do it: ✓ I want more practice: ‼

1 Listening. I can understand when people help me spell English words.

How do you spell *through*?

T – H – R – O – U – G – H

1	

2 Speaking. I can say what some things are made of.

This table's made of wood.

This bowl's made of glass.

2	

3 Reading. I can understand a recipe and use it to make some food.

Pizza

You need:
flour
salt   cheese
yeast   tomato
water   pepper

3	

4 Writing. I can write about my plans for a party, giving all the important information.

We're going to have a party in school. We can have it in ...

4	

I can ... Units 7 and 8

I can do it easily: ✓✓ I can do it: ✓ I want more practice: ‼
1
2
3
4

1  Listening. I can listen to a song and write the words in the spaces.

2 Speaking. I can say some things we should and shouldn't do to be healthy and help the planet.

You should brush your teeth every morning and night.

You shouldn't throw your garbage on the ground.

3 Reading. I can read and answer questions about different sports.

4 Writing. I can write about the sports that people in my class play and do.

People in our class play a lot of sports. They ...

Learning English: Outside the classroom

1 Do you do these things to improve your English? Write "yes" or "no" under the pictures.

Do homework ------

Read books and magazines ------

Find information on the computer ------

Listen to music ------

Review the class ------

Speak in English to people ------

Look for English around you!

2 Check (✓) the boxes when you find the information in English. What else can you find? Put the information in your Dossier.

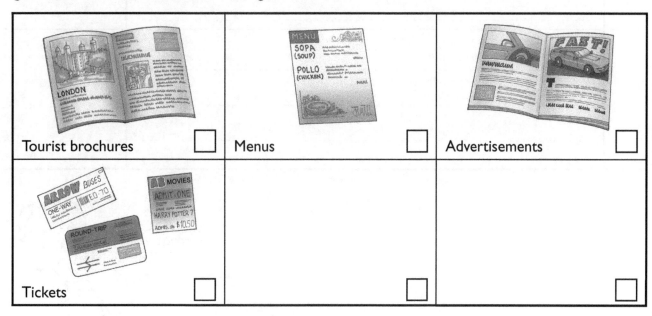

Tourist brochures ☐

Menus ☐

Advertisements ☐

Tickets ☐

☐

☐

My Dossier

The activities in the Dossier show what you can do in English. You can put some of your favorite work here, too. Write the titles and the dates you did the work below.

What can you do in English?

	Contents	Date
1	About me	
2	A city I know: _____	
3	How _____ is/are made.	
4	_____	
5	_____	
6	_____	
7	_____	
	_____ _____ _____	

Great work!

About me

Describe yourself, where you live, and your favorite activities and subjects. Draw or stick pictures in the boxes.

Description:

Where I live:

Activities and subjects I like:

More information: -----------------------------------

A city I know: _____

Describe your city or a city you visited. Draw or stick pictures in the boxes.

About the city in general:

Places you can go:

My opinion of this city:

Do you live in this city? _____

If not, when did you visit it? _____

What language(s) do they speak there? _____

How _____ is/are made

Do you know how paper is made? Do you know how cupcakes are made? Choose something we make. Draw pictures and write about it.

1 _____
_____
_____
_____

2 _____
_____
_____
_____

Where do we use this thing? _____

How important is it? Not very ☐   Fairly ☐   Very ☐   important.

Do you have this thing?   Yes ☐   No ☐

An endangered animal: _____

How many endangered animals do you know? Choose one to write about.
Draw or stick pictures in the boxes.

Description:

Where it lives, what it eats, etc.:

What can we do to save it?

Dossier ❖ Dossier ❖ Dossier ❖ Dossier ❖ Dossier ❖ Dossier

A sport I like: _____

Write about a sport you like. Draw or stick a picture in the frame.

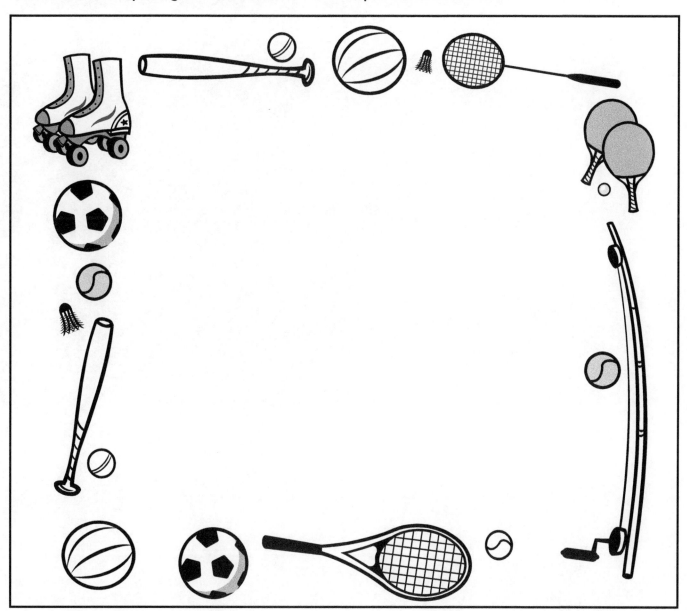

Where do you play/do it? _____
What do you need? _____
If it's a team sport, how many people play it? _____
What are the rules (what can you do and what can't you do)? _____
_____
_____
I play/do this sport: _____ I watch it on TV: _____
More information: _____

101

Thanks and Acknowledgments

Authors' thanks

Many thanks to everyone at Cambridge University Press and in particular to:

Rosemary Bradley, for overseeing the whole project and successfully pulling it all together with good humour; Fiona Davis, for her fine editorial skills; Colin Sage for his good ideas and helpful suggestions; Karen Elliott for her enthusiasm and creative reworking of the Phonics sections.

We would also like to thank all our students and colleagues at Star English, El Palmar, Murcia, and especially Jim Kelly and Julie Woodman for their help and suggestions at various stages of the project.

Dedications

For Carmen Navarro with love. Many thanks for all your hard work, help, and support over the years – CN

To my Murcian family: Adolfo and Isabel, the Peinado sisters and their other halves for always treating me so well, Thanks for being there and for making my life in Murcia so much fun – MT

The Authors and Publishers would like to thank the following teachers for their help in reviewing the material and for the invaluable feedback they provided:

Rocío Licea Ayala, Natalia Bitar, Diego Andres Gil Chibuque, Gayane Grigoryan, Shaun Sheahan, Gicela Ugalde.

We would also like to thank all the teachers who allowed us to observe their classes and who gave up their invaluable time for interviews and focus groups.

The authors and publishers acknowledge the following sources of copyright material and are grateful for the permissions granted. While every effort has been made, it has not always been possible to identify the sources of all the material used or to trace all copyright holders. If any omissions are brought to our notice, we will be happy to include the appropriate acknowledgments on reprinting.

p.6(1): Alamy/© Lennello Calvetti; p.6(2): Shutterstock/© Titov Dmitry; p.6(3): Alamy/© Steve Vidler; p.6(4,5,6): © Stephen Bond; p.9: Alamy/© The Print Collector; p.12(1): Rex Features/© Steve Meddle; p.12(2): Alamy/© Image Source; p.12(3): Shutterstock/© Nazarino; p.12(4): Shutterstock/© Florian Ispas; p.12(5): Getty Images/© AFP; p.12(6): Shutterstock/© Pavel Shchegolev p.20(1): Shutterstock/© Petronilo G. Dangoy JR; p.20(2): Shutterstock/© Dotshock; p.20(3): Shutterstock/© Kurhan; p.20(4): Alamy/© Keith Morris; p.20(5): Shutterstock/© Moshimochi; p.20(6): Shutterstock/© Ikonolast Fotografie; p.30(1): Alamy/© Larry Lilac; p.30(2): Shutterstock/© Pavell Photo & Video; p.30(3): Shutterstock/© Aboikis; p.30(4): Alamy/© Justin Kase zsixz; p.30(5): Shutterstock/© Cedric Weber; p.30(6): Alamy/© Guillem Lopez; p.38(1): Corbis/© Bettmann; p.38(2): Alamy/© GL Archive; p.38(3): Corbis/© Daniel Aguiler; p.38(4): Shutterstock/© Warren Goldswain; p.38(5): Getty Images; p.38(60: Shutterstock/© Barry Tuck; p.47: Alamy/© Robert Harding World Imagery; p.48(1): Used with kind permission of Réjeanne Arsenault; p.48(2): © Trustees of the British Museum; p.48(3): Alamy/© K-Photos; p.48(4): Press Association/© Rajanish Kakade/AP; p.48(5): Getty Images/© AFP; p.48(6): Shutterstock/© Blanscape; p.54: Shutterstock/© Gregdx; p.56(1,2): Shutterstock/© Danny Smythe; p.56(3,4,5): Shutterstock/© Alen Kadr; p.56(6): Shutterstock/© Andrey Kuzmin; p.60(a): © John Langdon 1996; p.60(c): © Rene Milot/Morgan Gaynin, Inc; p.66(1): Shutterstock/© Ecoprint; p.66(2): Shutterstock/© Scott E Read; p.66(3): Getty Images/EyeEm/Ahmed Nooh; p.66(4): Ardea/© Thomas Marent; p.66(5): Alamy/© Danita Delimont; p.73: Alamy/© Timothy Large; p.74(1,2): Shutterstock/© IM_Photo; p.74(3): Alamy/© Keith Morris; p.74(4): Getty Images/AFP/Lionel Bonaventure; p.74(5): Shutterstock/© Diego Barbieri; p.74(6): Shutterstock/© Vanessa Nel.

The authors and publishers are grateful to the following illustrators:

Moreno Chiacchiera, c/o Beehive; FLP; Graham Kennedy; Alan Rowe; Anthony Rule; Lisa Smith, c/o Sylvie Poggio; Jo Taylor, c/o Sylvie Poggio; Teresa Tibbetts, c/o Beehive; Gywneth Williamson

The publishers are grateful to the following contributors:

Stephen Bond: commissioned photography
Alison Prior: picture research
Wild Apple Design Ltd: page design
Lon Chan: cover design
John Green and Tim Woolf, TEFL Audio: audio recordings
Songs written and produced by Robert Lee, Dib Dib Dub studios.
John Marshall Media, Inc. and Lisa Hutchins: audio recordings for the American English edition
hyphen S.A.: publishing management, American English edition